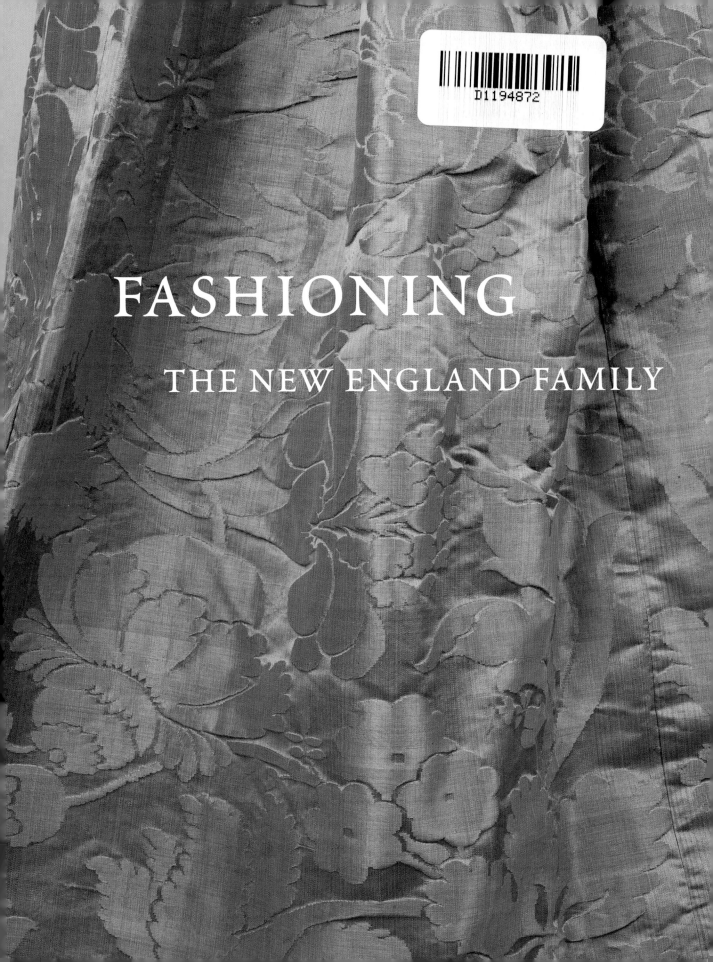

FASHIONING

THE NEW ENGLAND FAMILY

FASHIONING

THE NEW ENGLAND FAMILY

Kimberly S. Alexander

Based on the exhibition presented at
the Massachusetts Historical Society,
October 2018–April 2019

Published by
the Massachusetts Historical Society,
Boston | 2021

Distributed by the University of Virginia Press

Fashioning the New England Family, by Kimberly S. Alexander
Foreword by Anne E. Bentley

ISBN 978-1-936520-13-8

All original photographs of textiles are by Laura Wulf and © Massachusetts Historical Society, unless otherwise credited. All scanned collections are in the holdings of the Massachusetts Historical Society unless otherwise credited.

We are grateful to the Johns Hopkins University Press for permission to adapt for this publication portions of text that were published in Dr. Alexander's 2018 book, *Treasures Afoot: Shoe Stories from the Georgian Era*. The related passages appear in that volume on pages 11–13, 25, 44, 46–50, 53–56, 67–68, 71–73, 112–115, 123–124, 139–140, 148–151, and 160.

www.masshist.org

Opening pages:
FIG F.1 (half-title page): Detail, Rebecca Tailer Byles dress.
FIG F.2 (facing title page): Detail, Celadon green silk (dress with pelelrne cape).

Facing, FIGS F.1 and F.2: Byles dress and Celadon green silk (dress with pelelrne cape).

Following page spread:
FIGS F.3a, b: Pocketbook belonging to John Breed, 1732, Morocco.

IOHNBREED

1732

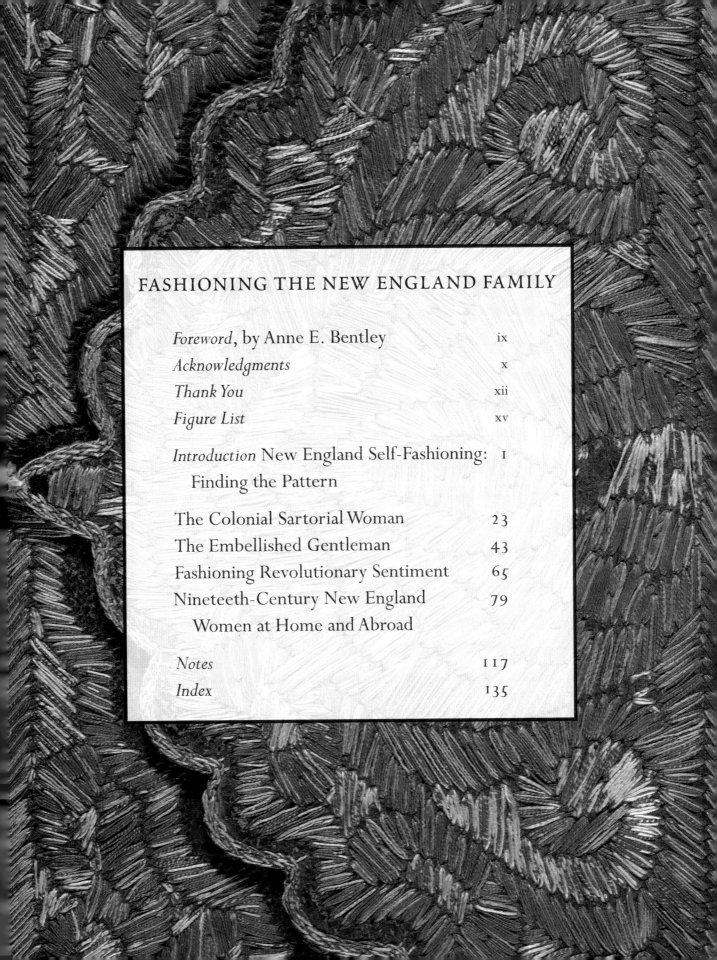

FASHIONING THE NEW ENGLAND FAMILY

FOREWORD

Anne E. Bentley,
Curator of Art, Massachusetts Historical Society

A Society has lately been instituted in this town, called the HISTORICAL SOCIETY; the professed design of which is, to collect, preserve and communicate, materials for a complete history of this country...

This phrase, from Jeremy Belknap's first sentence in his "Circular Letter of the Historical Society," is very familiar to those of us who work in the institution he and his associates founded in 1791: it has been our guiding purpose—indeed, our mission statement—from the very beginning. The remainder of that first sentence is less quoted: ". . . and accounts of all valuable efforts of human ingenuity and industry, from the beginning of its settlement." While Belknap's emphasis was on collecting printed and manuscript materials, he did make provision for "natural or artificial productions which may enlarge its museum." In Belknap's parlance, we may consider that the subjects of this book consist of artificial productions that uniquely help us tell part of the history of this country.

Of course Belknap never dreamed that clothing and personal accoutrement would, or could, provide historical applications beyond the immediate and obvious questions "who wore this

Facing page, FIG F.4: *Refashioning the New England Family* exhibition. Courtesy of Mary Sellner Orr.

Above, FIG F.5: Preparations in the Dowse Library. Courtesy of Anne E. Bentley.

and when?" I have worked with our "museum" objects for forty-eight years at this printing and must confess that I certainly had never approached our textiles as primary sources. It is my very good fortune to have assisted Kimberly S. Alexander as she researched for her book, *Treasures Afoot*. Her expertise is impressive and her enthusiasm so contagious that we quickly convinced her to sign on as our guest curator for the textile exhibition that accompanied this book.

From Dr. Alexander I have learned to follow not only the stitched, unstitched, and re-stitched seams in historical clothing for clues about their refashioning into the latest mode, but I have discovered that these pieces speak volumes when one considers the origins of some of their components – silks from the orient, dyes from all over the world, gold woven into lace from Europe. Endless questions flow when one takes time to look beyond the surface of these fascinating relics: who was exporting and shipping these textiles?, who was designing, cutting and sewing these clothes?, who had the money to lavish on these sumptuous articles?, what laws evolved around clothing and why?, how did embargos and war affect the various trades involved in textiles, clothing, and shoemaking? Why wigs? It has been an absolutely fascinating journey working with Kimberly and her colleagues in the world of textiles and their history. When you turn the page you will make your own discoveries and, like me, marvel at how eloquent these objects become under the expert guide of one who truly brings them to life.

ACKNOWLEDGMENTS

Every exhibition and publication has a backstory. This particular story started with the search for a shoe—a pair of Georgian wedding shoes worn by Bostonian Rebecca Tailer Byles in 1747, to be exact. Curator Anne Bentley and I first met at the Massachusetts Historical Society in 2015, and since that time, we have had many opportunities to look at countless examples of fine textiles, costumes, and accessories held in the Art and Artifact Collection. We found the green silk damask shoes, we looked at gowns, waistcoats, a wig, and much more. We began the process of knitting together the artifacts with their text-based documents, especially letters, diary entries, and newspaper accounts. The materials range from the seventeenth century to the early twentieth century, and the lengthy process of examining the garments and investigating their family histories yielded a fellowship, an exhibition, and, finally, the book you hold in your hands. We have enjoyed every step of this journey and are honored to share it with you as you read.

The project would not have been possible without the vision of two executive officers of the MHS—Pres. Dennis Fiori, now emeritus, and Pres. Catherine Allgor. The support they gave this project from day one, in combination with that of the Board of Trustees, was full and unstinting. We would like to thank all our colleagues at the Massachusetts Historical Society. They cheerfully encouraged, supported, and assisted in bringing this exhibition and publication to completion, especially Carol Knauff, Sarah Bertulli, and Gavin Kleespies. Above all, we are indebted to Ondine E. Le Blanc, Jim Connolly, Agnieszka Rec, and Tess Renault, as well as intern Emily Luong, for editing, designing, and shepherding this book through to publication.

Their dedication to excellence and the craft of history shine from every page.

Colleagues here and elsewhere also provided vital research assistance. At the MHS, we benefited from the expertise of Mary Yacovone, the excellent reference librarians, and editors of the Adams Papers edition, as well as the volunteer efforts of Reed A. Gochberg, Rachael Barrett, and Danay Vera. We are likewise indebted to the efforts of our colleagues Dale Valena and Astrida Schaeffer, of the University of New Hampshire Museum and Schaeffer Arts; Janea Whitacre, Christina Johnson, Rebecca Starkins, and Sarah Woodyard of the Colonial Williamsburg Foundation, Margaret Hunter Shop Milliners and Mantua Makers; and Betty Myers, Debbie Turpin, Sara Palmer, and Regina Blizzard—Master, Journeymen, and Apprentice in the Colonial Williamsburg Foundation Wig Shop; Nathaniel Sheidley, Director, and Sira Dooley Fairchild, Collections Manager, of Revolutionary Spaces (Bostonian Society); and Kelly Cobble, Curator of the Adams National Historical Park.

While the bulk of photographs were taken by talented MHS photographer Laura Wulf, we are appreciative of illustrations provided by Revolutionary Spaces, Nicole McAllister, Special Collections Librarian; Museum of Fine Arts, Boston; National Portrait Gallery, Smithsonian Institution; the Oliver Family; Peabody Essex Museum; Philadelphia Museum of Art; Mary Sellner Orr; and Camille Breeze, Museum Textile Services, with photos by Morgan Blei Carbone; and the Metropolitan Museum of Art, which generously makes press quality images of many of its collections freely available online with a Creative Commons license.

We are deeply grateful to the generosity of our Kickstarter donors who believed in this project and who stayed committed to it despite the delays that accompanied its completion. Finally, we wish to thank our families, friends, and the scholars and researchers who we hope will find insight and inspiration for their own work perusing these pages.

—*Kimberly S. Alexander and Anne E. Bentley*

thank you

KICKSTARTER

FUNDERS

Sara Georgini
Juliana Goodwin
Ruth Ann Graime
Hannah Gravius
Vickie Green
Anne Gwin
Emilie Haertsch
Ann B. Hamilton
Susan K. Harmon
Franchesca V Havas
Nicole M. Hayes
Theresa Hitch
Ruth Hodges and John
  LeClaire
Susan Holloway Scott
Jeffrey Hopper
Pauline Hsieh
Barbara Housh
Sharon E. Huffstetler
Carol J. Hutchinson
Janith
Nancy K. Johnson
Lynn Jones
Jordana
Sophie Kaiser
Rebecca Kemp Brent
Spencer D. C. Keralis,
  Ph.D.
Kristine Kilkenny
Rachael Kinnison, Lady's
  Repository Museum
Amy Kitmacher
Gavin W. Kleespies
Joady Knoebel Gorelick
Laurie LaBar
Dr. Vicki L. Lamb
Donna Langworthy
Karen U. Lavoie
Sharon Leloup
Patricia C. Loesch

Laura D. Loucas
In loving memory of
  Justine Luongo
Jaclyn M
Elisabeth Magid
Marcy Mahle
Mary Corbet's
  Needle 'n Thread
Mary Eileen Mangan
Catherine T. Massey
Meghan A. McClafferty
M. McMath
Susan E. McTigue
Pamela Meyer
Ellen W. Miller
Marla R. Miller
Neal Millikan
MLR
Teresa Mogensen
Dane A. Morrison
Britney Mortenson
Robert D. Mussey, Jr.
Patti Myers
Elizabeth Nagle
Lisa Nurme
Amelia O'Donnell
Janet A. Ottman
Laura C. Owen
Christine Pascoe
The Paull Family
Lisa Pearson and
  Catherine Iannuzzo
Mrs Diane Pegler
Cassidy Percoco
P E Petrik
Elisabethe Phipps
Beth Pinterich
Mallory Anne Porch
Robin Portune
Barbara Reaveley

Meaghan M. Reddick
Patricia Richards
Debbie Richey
Robert G. Ripley, Jr.
Julia and Stephen
  Roberts
Nancy L. Robinson
Shere'e Robinson
Jason Rodriguez
Patricia Rogers
Rachel Rogers-Rodgers
Diana Habra Rotheneder
Laura D. Rubin
Diane Rudin
Nicole Rudolph
Wendy Salisbury Howe
Astrida Schaeffer
Alice Alane Scott
Chastity Senek
Cynthia Settje
Jenny Shaffer
Taylor Shelby
Barbara Singer
Mary-Denise Smith
Sabra Smith
Patricia Smith-Gardner
Carolyn Standing Webb
Stephanie St. Clair
David and Cynthia
  Steinhoff
Lydia Stevenson
Susan Stewart
Rebecca and Matthew
  Theerman
Thistle Threads
Marjie Thompson
Mary V. Thompson
Ursula Thompson
Stacey Thoyre
Christene Thurston

Rebecca M. Valleskey
Mary Van Tyne
Danay Vera
Kristen Von Malder
Tara Vose Raiselis
Deborah Wade
Abigail Weiner
Wenham Museum
Katy Werlin
Louise West
Kathleen E. Weston
Stacy C. Whittaker
Abigail Wilcox
Audrey J. Wolfe
Missy Wolfe
Chris Woodyard
Mary E. Yacovone
Evan W. Zajdel

Facing page, FIG F.6:
Clockwise from bottom:
Rebecca Parker Farrar's
wedding shoes, ca. 1819;
Elizabeth Dennison's
wedding shoes, 1859;
Sarah Leverett Tuttle's
dancing shoe and
wedding shoe, 1860s.

FIGURE LIST

S F.7, F.8

INTRODUCTION

Front view of
Byles family
dress, photograph
by Morgan Blei
Carbone, Museum
Textile Services,
courtesy of
Camille Breeze.

Oil on canvas, 1688, painted in England
MHS: Artwork 01.175

CH 1: COLONIAL SARTORIAL WOMAN

CH 3: REVOLUTIONARY SENTIMENT

3.1   64

George Washington, portrait attributed to Jane Stuart
Oil on canvas, 19th century
MHS: Artwork 01.312
Painter Jane Stuart, of Boston, Mass., and Newport, R.I., supported the family by reproducing portraits by her father, Gilbert Stuart, such as this after the "Athenaeum Washington."

3.2a, b   67

Fabric samples for Col. Dwight, by way of Capt. Hollowell.
Unidentified correspondent to merchant Henry Leddel. Wove paper folio sheet, red printing ink, felted wool, iron gall ink. Undated.
MHS: Textiles—Fabrics 039

3.3   68

Elizabeth Price memorandum book, 1775
MHS: Price-Osgood-Valentine Papers, Ms. N-2199

3.4   71

Abigail Adams to John Adams, July 16, 1775
MHS: Adams Family Papers

3.5   72, 73

Hancock family purse, open
Silk damask with gold thread, late 18th or early 19th century, Boston, Mass.
MHS: Textiles—Pocketbooks 021
The silk of this drawstring pouch is believed to have come from the lining of a coat that belonged to Thomas Hancock, who raised John Hancock, his nephew.
See also Fig. I.8.

3.6   73

Piece of dress fabric, Hancock family
Silk brocade, 18th century
MHS: Textiles—Fabrics 026

3.7   74

William Dawes leather pouch
Kidskin, paper label, late 18th century, Marlborough, Mass.
MHS: Pocketbooks 027
The full text reads, "This bag contains Sundrey Deeds &c.—& Notes of hand considered of little, or no, Value—belonging to the Estate of William Dawes Jr., Esqu. late of Marlborough dec'd Feby 25th 1799—other papers relating to the business of said dec'd which were decidedly of no consequence were this day burned Feby. 28, 1817."

3.8   75

Dawes family blue checked cloth
Cotton, indigo dye, late 18th or early 19th century, attributed to Lucretia Dawes, [New Hampshire]
MHS: Fabrics 036

3.9   77

Hannah Dawes Newcomb muff
Silk, multicolored silk thread, late 18th to early 19th century, [Massachusetts]
MHS: Needlework Misc 009
Remade from another item and embroidered by Hannah Dawes Newcomb

3.10   78

Fabric from a dress belonging to Elizabeth Pierpont
Silk, silk thread, late 18th century, English (possibly Spitalfields) or French
MHS: Textiles—Fabrics 021

3.11   79

Silk scarf, Hartwell-Clark family
Silk, gold thread, [18--]
MHS: Textiles—Hartwell-Clark 018

CH 4: 19TH-CENTURY NEW ENGLAND WOMEN

4.1a   80

Lap quilt (detail), with a portrait of Rachel Smith Bagley Clark and letter from Ella Hartwell to Hilda Pfeiffer
Silk, cotton, cotton thread, 1868, Rachel Smith Bagley Clark, Watertown, Mass.
MHS: Textiles—Hartwell-Clark 101
Made by Rachel Smith Bagley Clark for Rachael Clark Hartwell Pfeiffer

4.2a-e 82, 83

State Street, 1801, by James Brown Marston
Oil on canvas, 1801, American
MHS: Artwork 02.007

4.3   84

Empire silhouette dress
Cotton, linen, 1800-1805, American
Brooklyn Museum Costume Collection at The Metropolitan Museum of Art, Gift of the Brooklyn Museum, 2009; Gift of the Jason and Peggy Westerfield Collection, 1969. Accession Number: 2009.300.3328.

4.4   85

Elizabeth Price memorandum book, 1804
MHS: Price-Osgood-Valentine Papers, Ms. N-2199

4.5   86

Satin gown belonging to Abigail Adams
Satin, self fabric trim, ca. 1800, [English?]; with alterations by the family as late as 1820
Adams National Historical Park, National Park Service: catalog #8301. Photograph courtesy of Kimberly S. Alexander.
This dress appears to be the one in the portrait by Gilbert Stuart, painted in Washington between 1800 and 1815. The earliest date attributed to the dress comes from Adams's granddaughter Elizabeth Coombs Adams, who identified it as "worn by Mrs. John Adams in London in 1786." As origi-nally conceived, the gown appears to have had a low neckline filled in with a white fabric ending in a double-frilled collar with lace trim. Elizabeth also noted that she wore the gown herself, probably for a costume ball, and it was likely altered to its present state at that time.

4.6   87

Abigail Smith Adams, by Gilbert Stuart
Oil on canvas, 1800/1815, American
Gift of Mrs. Robert Homans, Accession Number 1954.7.2. Courtesy National Gallery of Art, Washington.

4.7   88

Dimity pocket belonging to Abigail Adams
Dimity, cotton tapes, late 18th-early 19th century, [Massachusetts]
MHS: Textiles—Clothing, women's 008

4.8   88

Note, Elizabeth Coombs Adams
Before 1903
Arrived with Fig. 4.7.

4.9   90

Embroidered pocket, ca. 1784
Cotton, wool, ca. 1784, American
Brooklyn Museum Costume Collection at The Metropolitan Museum of Art, Gift of the Brooklyn Museum, 2009; Bequest of Marie Bernice Bitzer, by exchange, 1996. Accession Number: 2009.300.2241

4.10   90

Purse, Leverett family
Silk, silk thread, 1840, New Hampshire, Harriet Leverett
MHS: Pocketbooks 020
Made for Sarah Dutton Leverett Tuttle. An accompanying note reads, "Embroidery done for S. D. Leverett by her Aunt Harriet Leverett in eighteen forty—for a muff."

4.11   91

Dress, gigot sleeves
Cotton, linen, 1832-1835, American

Brooklyn Museum Costume Collection at The Metropolitan Museum of Art, Gift of the Brooklyn Museum, 2009; Gift of Mrs. Harold N. Weber, 1990. Accession Number: 2009.300.578a, b

4.12   92

Dress with pelerine cape
Silk, silk thread, 1830s; likely altered, 1840s
MHS: Textiles—Clothing, women's 001
See also Fig. F.2 and page 108.

4.13   95

Textile sample book
Commercial indigo cotton samples made and sold by the Merrimack Manufacturing Company of Lowell, Mass. Embossed paper folder with outside label "M.M.C. /A." Inner folder has a ca. 1850 engraving titled "Merrimack Prints, Lowell, Mass." Folder contains 19 samples of indigo and white cotton with allover small designs.
MHS: Textiles—Fabrics 035

4.14   96

Stockings, embellished by Harriet (Nelson) Leverett
Silk machine-knit stockings, silk thread, ca. 1834, European
MHS: Textiles—Leverett 001

4.15   97

Socks, embellished by Harriet (Nelson) Leverett
Silk machine-knit socks, silk thread, ca. 1834, European
MHS: Textiles—Leverett 005

4.16   98

Mourning dress (bodice, sleeve), Sarah Dutton Leverett Tuttle
Silk, buckram lining, 1840, attributed to Caroline H. Leverett or Harriet Leverett
MHS: Textiles—Leverett 013

4.17   99

Viault-Esté of Paris shoes, both belonging to Sarah Leverett

Silk, kidskin, lace, silk ribbon, [1860s], French
MHS: Textiles—Shoes 003 (wedding shoe), Textiles—Shoes 004 (dancing shoe)
See also Fig. F.6.

4.18   100

Portrait of Rachael Hartwell Pfeiffer, 1903
Memoria in Aeterna (privately printed), text by Theodora Kyle Chase, dedicated to Hilda from her grandmother. Portrait appears two pages after the title page.
MHS: Hartwell-Clark Family Papers, Memorial Book, 1905

4.19   101

Evening gown belonging to Rachael Hartwell Pfeiffer
Bodice: Silk, silk crepe, silk thread, lace, artificial pearls and brilliants, [1892], American
MHS: Textiles—Hartwell-Clark 100
See also page 108.

4.20   102

Lace triangle with scalloped edge
Cotton, late 19th century
MHS: Textiles—Hartwell-Clark 034

4.21   104

Rachael Hartwell Pfeiffer letter journals, 1890s
MHS: Hartwell-Clark Family Papers, Mount Tabor Chronicle, Volume II

4.22   105

Sketch of fishwife
[Watercolor?], July 22, 1899, Rachael Hartwell Pfeiffer
MHS: Hartwell-Clark Family Papers, Tour of Holland, 7 July-August 1899

4.23, 4.19, 4.12   108

Dresses on display at exhibition
Left to right: Rachael Hartwell Pfeiffer wedding dress; same, evening dress; provenance unknown, 1830s dress with pelerine cape.
Courtesy of Mary Sellner Orr.

Following page spread:

FIG F.9: Detail, textile sample book,
Merrimack Manufacturing Company
of Lowell.

FIG I.0: Detail, Frederic Baury vest.

FASHIONING

THE NEW ENGLAND FAMILY

NEW ENGLAND SELF-FASHIONING—
UNDERSTANDING THE PATTERN

FOUNDED IN 1791, the Massachusetts Historical Society came into existence for the express purpose of preserving the manuscript record of the American Revolution—at that moment a series of events still fresh in the minds of most New Englanders. Colonial and Revolutionary-era manuscripts made up the heart of its initial collection, supplemented in ensuing decades with an enormous quantity of nineteenth-century documents, largely gathered in family collections carrying names recognizable from the historical and literal landscape of New England, such as Winthrop, Adams, Quincy, Hancock, Saltonstall, Revere, Leverett, Boylston, Oliver, Bromfield, and Byles.

Clearly, these collected papers primarily come from political, economic, and social leaders, but manuscript records can still yield much evidence of less prominent lives. This is less true, however, of the surviving objects of everyday life—chairs and desks, jewelry and eyeglasses, watches and waistcoats—that have made their way into the Society's holdings, many of which arrived alongside family papers. As we might expect, the textiles, garments, and accessories housed at the MHS largely represent the by-gone wardrobes of elite ladies and gentlemen. This effect repeats itself in archives, museums, and historic house collections throughout the original British colonies. The material culture that remains does so because of the resources of families who could afford to purchase high-quality items, to pass them with great care from generation to generation, and to donate them for cultural heritage purposes.

As such, for the most part, the items studied in this volume, and gathered for the exhibition it supplements, tell us about the lifestyles of New England families who occupied the pinnacle of the early American social fabric. This bounty, however skewed, is reflected in the examinations undertaken here. It also reflects the two-fold function of clothing in many cultures across time and around the globe: as a utilitarian protective layer and as a form of communication. The latter expresses many aspects of an individual's relationship to social condition, including status, power, taste, politics, and social function, among many other relevant facets. Largely a by-product of wealth, each item represented here shows concretely what wealth could command in its era—the materials, the workmanship, the global trade routes, the fashionability.

I.1a: Detail,
lace.

The eighteenth century was an age of consumption throughout Europe, especially concentrated in busy and wealthy cities like London and Paris. It was similarly, if on a different scale, an age of consumption in the hubs of English America. In *A History of Colonial America*, Max Savelle and Robert Middlekauff enumerated the trade as precisely as possible, asserting that

> in 1768, which was perhaps the last normal year before the Revolution, goods traded of the continental colonies with the mother country totaled (in pounds sterling) 3,408,702 of which (in pounds sterling) 2,157,248 were in imports from her and (in pounds sterling) 1,251,451 were in exports to her.[1]

A majority of the textiles used in America between 1740 and 1770 were imported to the colonies either directly or indirectly from England. In fact, America was one of the biggest markets for British textiles.[2] To colonial Americans, proud of their Britishness but also eager to demonstrate their own wherewithal and solid social standing, a garment or an accessory that demonstrated access to that market was a prized possession. While the derivation of goods from England invoked a sense of British identity, the derivation of goods from other sources around the world demonstrated America's place in the global maritime economy.[3] Both were important.

The cost of clothing, at all levels of quality, demanded resources. Before the mechanization of textile production, even utilitarian garments and accessories were an investment. The supply chain that brought an item to the consumer was not simple. Each element that went into an article of clothing—typically fabric, thread, dye, and fasteners, as well as embellishments such as lace—made a metaphorical journey from initial cultivation of the raw resource (such as silk worms or cotton plants for cloth, and plants like indigofera or insects like the cochineal for dyes) to processing and fabrication. The literal journey of an item could move it halfway around the globe, beginning in Asia or Africa, passing through Europe and landing in England, before a sailing ship brought it across the Atlantic to a wharf in Boston, where it might turn up in a shop in town.

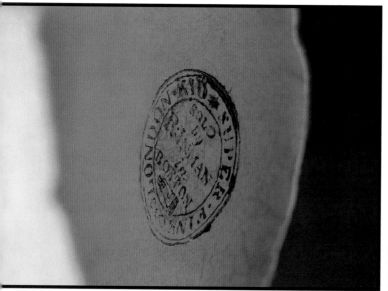

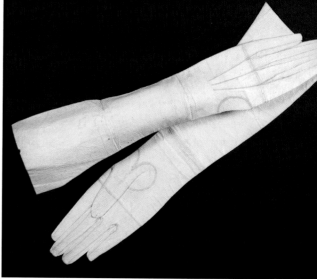

The price put on an item depended on many factors, but that journey from raw material to the finished product for consumers was a key one. In New England culture, as in English culture, the most desirable textiles were often those that were the most difficult to obtain, derived from the rarest origins. Displaying one's ability to own such materials was a powerful signal of wealth and status. Silk, one of the most coveted textiles in early modern Europe, illustrates that dynamic between supply and demand.[4]

Silk appears again and again in the garments that have survived over centuries, cared for in museum collections, treasured because it exemplified luxury. It may be hard to imagine that this lustrous material is the product of caterpillars, the tiny larvae of silkworm moths. Notoriously difficult to care for, the larvae spin cocoons, each one of which is made of a single strand of silk—the raw beginning of the highly prized commodity. The production of the textile, first developed in China, was complex and labor intensive, demanded proper care for both the silkworms and mulberry trees that they depended on for food. Creating fabrics from the strands required artisans with specialized knowledge, including how to set up looms and design the patterns for the weaving, as did dyeing both the threads and the textile.

FIG I.2a, b: Women's gloves and detail of label. Made in London and sold in Boston, ca. 1760s. Ink stamp inside cuff reads, "SUPER FINE LONDON KID / SOLD by R: INMAN in BOSTON."

FIG I.3: Swatch of damask silk. One of three late 18th-century fragments from a dress worn by Elizabeth Pierpont (later Cunningham). This crimson, floral damask is a good match to Chinese examples from the period.

For thousands of years, the ability to produce silk remained mostly in the East, while its value as an export spread westward to Europe. The possibility of also exporting the resources needed to make this lucrative commodity attracted considerable attention in the West. Although not every climate could support sericulture, competitors to China's millennia-long monopoly emerged along the Silk Road, where information about its manufacture traveled with the textile, across Central Asia and into Europe. For a time, Constantinople (Istanbul) succeeded, but with the city's fall in the thirteenth century, thousands of artisans, whose expertise had made the industry possible, journeyed abroad in search of new opportunities. As these workers moved westward, centers of silk production strengthened throughout the Italian peninsula. Cities such as Lucca, Genoa, Venice, and Florence were well positioned to meet the growing demand for silk among the rich and powerful of Europe. The French also established a successful silk industry, based in Lyon, in the sixteenth century. However, while some western nations could support small pockets of both silk production and weaving, few succeeded at large-scale export of the raw commodity. As a result, in the seventeenth and eighteenth centuries, China remained the primary exporter of both raw and finished silk.[5]

The potential for domestic production in England looked promising late in the seventeenth century, when hundreds of thousands of French Protestants known as Huguenots, many of whom were skilled weavers and experts in sericulture, immigrated to England to escape religious persecution. Some areas, most notably Spitalfields in London, gave rise to the establishment of exceptional workshops for designing and weaving silk.[6] However, England's climate largely prevented the domestic production of raw silk from achieving any measurable success.

Of course, many English investors had also eyed the new colonies in America as possible sites for supporting a British silk industry—one of the hoped for results of colonization from the outset. As early as 1613, under the reign of King James, Virginia received its first supply of silkworms for cultivation; it would be fifteen years before that investment resulted in a batch of silk. In the ensuing decades, Virginians were increasingly ordered and enticed to cultivate the mulberry trees and the worms needed to produce more raw silk thread, which would then be sent to England for dying and weaving. Similar efforts continued into the eighteenth century and across the colonies, but production never became robust.[7] There were instances of success, such as in Pennsylvania, thanks to Benjamin Franklin, who promoted sericulture throughout his career; Connecticut, where there was sustained silk production for two hundred years;

South Carolina, where Eliza Lucas Pinckney was an advocate; and Georgia.[8]

The eighteenth-century North American market for silken textiles still depended on imports, of course, and it served consumers who appreciated the variety of weaves importers made available, from taffeta, satin, and velvet to richly woven damasks and brocades. Both damask and brocade were woven with distinctive techniques that displayed their "figures" differently: in a damask, typically made of one yarn in one color, the complete pattern would show on both sides of the cloth, albeit in reverse; in a brocade, comprising several yarns in two or more colors, the complete pattern would show only on one side.

Just as elite consumers in New England enjoyed access to high-end silks from China, England, Italy, and France, often by way of English agents, they were also accustomed to other quality goods from around the globe, including many types of wool, one of the favorites being calamanco, finished primarily in Norwich, England; cotton, which grew around the world—but only minimally in North America before the nineteenth century—and was, similarly, processed in many locales; and linen, made from flax, also grown and processed in many regions. Leather other than deerskin, which could be easily obtained in America, often came from Britain, Spain, or North Africa (typically referred to as *Morocco leather*). For embellishments, shoppers could choose among metallic threads, used to create a desirable trim known as *lace*; a silk knotted trimming known as *floss* or *fly fringe*; and spangles, much like sequins, often used on hand-embroidered textiles.

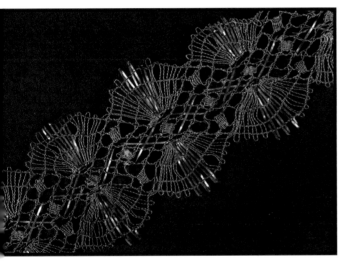

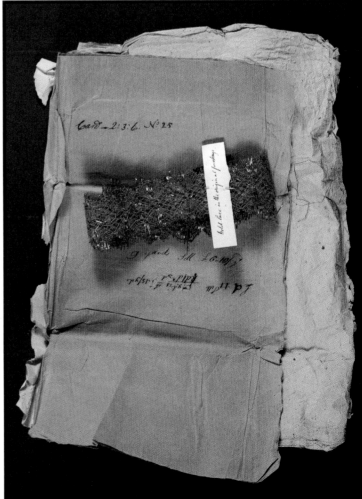

acing page, FIG I.4: Byles family dress, Revolutionary era, nade of silk that is most likely French.

his page, FIG I.1b, c: Upham family gold lace, detail and with ackaging. Handcrafted bobbin lace made from twisted and at gold wire. Stored in original laid paper wrapper. Pencil ote on outer wrap reads, "Gold lace give me with other old-ashioned things by my mother. A. S. U."

In a 1741 newspaper advertisement from Philadelphia, we can see the relative values these textiles carried in a colonial market—and especially the place of silk. In the November 12, 1741, issue of the *American Weekly Mercury*, Philadelphia shopkeeper George House announced that he had silk, wool, and leather shoes for sale:

> Variety of choice neat women shoes with both Russell, Cloath, Callimanco and Morocco; Golloshoes black and red, very neat clogs with Morocco and Sattin Tyes, all at 6/6 per pair. Pattern shoes at 7 shillings and silk from 15 to 18 shillings per pair. Also good live geese feathers, and sundry other goods very cheap.[9]

Shoes made of calamanco, which had a glazed finish created when the wool was passed through rollers at a high temperature, were priced less than seven shillings. The silk shoes were at least double, in cases almost triple, the cost of those fashioned from any other material.

Dye, as well as fabric, could contribute to a garment's value in the marketplace. Dyes that derived from less abundant resources and more complex production processes could signal the elevated status of the owner, as did deep indigo, Tyrian purple, the bright yellow typically known as *Chinese* or *imperial yellow*, and the prized cochineal red.[10] The name of the latter, in fact, comes from the insects that are dried and crushed to yield the pigment used for the dye. Its route to an eighteenth-century New England consumer involved two transatlantic crossings: originating in Mexico, the pigment traveled to Europe for use as a dye there; the finished textiles destined for the American market then moved westward again.[11] In his *Fable of the Bees* (1723–1724), English satirist Bernard de Mandeville took the reader on a whirlwind tour of the labor required to attain such a desirable color:

What a Bustle is there to be made in several Parts of the World, before a fine Scarlet or crimson Cloth can be produced, what Multiplicity of Trades and Artificers must be employ'd! Not only such as are obvious, as Wool-combers, Spinners, the Weaver, the Cloth-worker, the Scourer, the Dyer, the Setter, the Drawer and the Packer; but others that are more remote and might seem foreign to it; as the Millwright, the Pewterer and the Chymist, which yet are all necessary as well as a great Number of other Handicrafts to have the Tools, Utensils and other Implements belonging to the Trades already named: But all these things are done at home, and may be perform'd without extraordinary Fatigue or Danger; the most frightful Prospect is left behind, when we reflect on the Toil and Hazard that are to be undergone Abroad, the vast Seas we are to

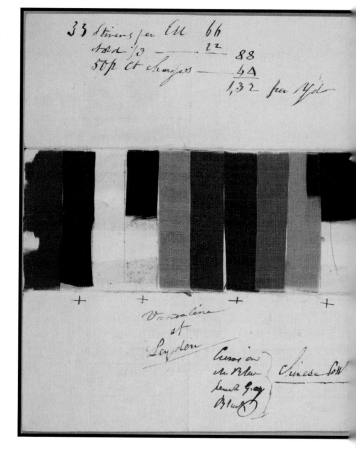

go over, the different Climates we must be obliged to endure, and the several Nations we must be obliged to for their Assistance.[12]

Compiling further hazards endured to acquire cochineal and similar dyes, Mandeville reached his charge that it all held "no other Reason, than the Satisfaction a Man receives from having a Garment made of Scarlet or Crimson Cloth."

But it was apparently all worth it, judging by this exchange between John and Abigail Adams regarding a scarlet cloth that could have been the result of a cochineal-based dye. While John was in Europe as an American minister, he wrote to Abigail from The Hague in October 1782 to boast of the textiles he had found to send home:

> I have Sent you an whole Piece of most excellent and beautiful Scarlet Cloth—it is very Saucy. 9 florins almost a Guinea a Dutch ell, much less than an English Yard. I have sent some blue too very good. Give *your Boys* a suit of Cloths if you will or keep enough for it some years hence and your-self and *Daughter* a Ridinghood in honour of the Manufactures of Haerlem. The Scar-let is "croisée" as they call it. You never saw such a Cloth.[13]

Of course, not every New England woman had a personal agent choosing expertly dyed fabrics at European markets for her; most who could afford the best dyes depended on expert local artisans to prepare and apply the fashionable pigments to their valuable textiles. This de-mand could provide a thriving customer base for skilled dyers, as James Vincent surely knew when he placed a notice in a 1729 issue of the *New England Weekly Journal*. Promising to provide

FIG I.6: Abigail Adams, by Benjamin Blyth. See Fig. 2.2 for Blyth portrait of John Adams.

FIG I.7: Pocketbook belonging to Benjamin Stuart, dated 1753, with a yellow silk lining. See Fig. 2.9.

ft, FIG I.5: Sample folder of Chinese textiles for sale through Dutch merchant, 18th century, with notes about cost and lors penned in English.

"best and newest manor, at reasonable rates for ready money," Vincent also stressed that he had learned his trade in London.[14] Of course, not everyone could afford to take their clothing to be "dipt" or refreshed with expensive dyes, and there were less pricey plant and animal dyes in widespread use, including for use at home. Typically these produced colors that faded more quickly or that were not as bright as those employed by a professional.[15]

In the seventeenth, eighteenth, and early nineteenth centuries, New England shoppers had choices, depending on cost, about how much labor to put into making their clothes. Even well-to-do women in the eighteenth century sometimes still worked clothes at home, and anyone inclined to sew or finish their own clothes was likely to purchase the components of a garment to be "made up" at home, while other consumers might purchase the pieces and take them to a local dressmaker or tailor.[16] Petticoats, for example, were often shipped in parts or whole cloth and then fitted and stitched together after they arrived at their final destinations. Alternatively, a dressmaker or home seamstress could make a bespoke petticoat to match an ensemble. Petticoat construction was relatively simple, and the distinction of the finished piece really depended on the quality of the textile or the embellishment lavished upon it.[17]

Some of the best extant examples of "ready made" (as opposed to custom made) clothing are men's waistcoats, which in the eighteenth century were typically sold in pieces, as "fronts" or "panels." This made it easier for embroiderers to do their work, which was done on a frame, possibly before export. For example, William Tailer's embroidery was most likely completed in England or France by anonymous, but skilled, women workers who were paid a trifle per

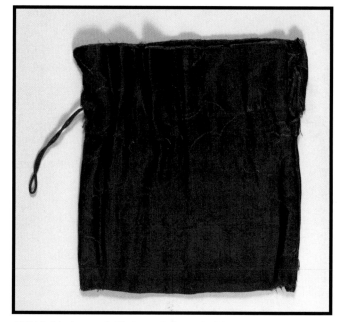

FIG I.8: Made up of silk damask from an older garment, this Hancock family pouch, probably late 18th century, shows the strong color-fastness of a high-quality dye. See Fig. 3.5 for more images of this item.

piece. The use of pre-fabricated panels also made it easier for the tailor to fit the garment to the wearer upon purchase. In addition to waistcoat fronts, the buyer could select the type of back he wanted. While backs were generally linen or a similar simple cloth, those who wanted to be exceedingly extravagant might choose a costly material or even an embroidered back—despite the fact that a gentleman would not have appeared in public without a coat over his waistcoat. Alternatively, some waistcoats were completed and then shipped to America for purchase in a shop or from a tailor, while a very fashionable and well-resourced gentleman might have a waistcoat entirely custom made to accompany a suit of clothes.

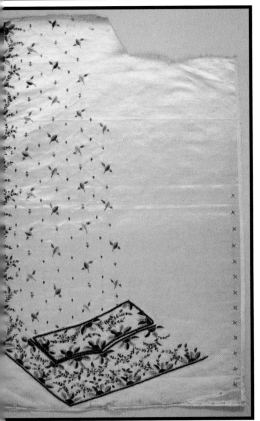

Above, FIG I.9a: William Tailer waistcoat, detail. The variation and intricacy of the design show that it is a high-end piece. See Fig. 2.10 and pages 52-53 for a full description.

Left, FIG I.10: Example of a waistcoat panel for the "ready made" market. Waistcoat panel (left), silk, ca. 1780, probably British. The Metropolitan Museum of Art, New York, Purchase, Irene Lewisohn Bequest, 1966, Accession Number: C.I.66.59.1b.

WHAT WAS FASHIONABLE in the British world changed over the centuries, and the style adopted by a mid-eighteenth-century Boston lady or gentleman was quite removed from the starting points of English settlement, especially in New England. The nascent colonies of the 1620s and 1630s, Plimoth Plantation and the Massachusetts Bay Colony (MBC) respectively, could produce little of their own materials for clothing, let alone anything that would be considered high-end in a European city. At the start, shipments of goods to the colonies were relatively small and tended to necessity. However, the limitations of production and shipping were not the only determining factors on sartorial conventions in early New England: at that time, self-fashioning was shaped at least as much by ideology.

The greater part of the colonists who arrived in these first decades had been spurred to cross the Atlantic by their religious principles, seeking a refuge from the religious strife that was fracturing England. In the early sixteenth century, when Henry VIII broke with the Catholic Church and put the Church of England under the control of the monarch, that schism created decades of conflict between English Catholics and Protestants. Over the next century, power shifted back and forth between the denominations, usually depending on the religious affinities of the ruler, and each shift was often marked by violence and persecution. Even with Protestant monarchs—Elizabeth I and James I—on the throne in the first decades of the seventeenth century, the continuing conflict made life difficult for religious dissenters who charged that the Church of England did not go far enough in distinguishing itself from Catholicism by adopting the more "pure" practices of religious reformation.

The conflict erupted in civil war in 1642, after years of tension between Charles I, who was perceived as too sympathetic to Catholicism, and the dissenters who, politically and militarily, were led by Oliver Cromwell, a Puritan. The contest between these forces continued until Charles I was captured, tried for treason, and beheaded in 1649. For the next decade, Parliament and Cromwell, as Lord Protector, governed England, giving authority to Puritan religious practice as well. In 1660, not long after Cromwell's death, the monarchy was restored as Charles II, the son and heir of Charles I, took the throne. His reign also established a more moderate doctrine for the Church of England.

The enemy lines in this war had followed religious differences but also largely adhered to class distinctions: the king's forces, referred to as *royalists* or *cavaliers*, were drawn largely from the landed gentry and minor nobility; many of Cromwell's followers, often called *Roundheads* or *parliamentarians*, were merchants and skilled tradesmen, drawn from the middle and laboring classes.[18] The differences also played out in the attire that became typical of each faction. The term *cavalier* came to denote not just the men who supported the king but also their attire, akin to the styles worn at courts in Europe and especially in Catholic countries. These costumes dazzled the eye with richly colored and lustrous fabrics, faceted with an abundance of pleats and dripping with eye-catching embellishments. This fashion was even reflected in some clothing worn at the English settlements in Virginia, which preceded those in New England and were not established by religious dissenters. "These refugees arrived in Virginia bedecked in their best ribbons and laces," notes historian Mary Doering, "flaunting

FIG I.11a: Detail of a 17th-century fan, European, owned by Bostonian Anthony Stoddard. See Fig. I.11b (p. 20) for full image.

their clothing as a badge of allegiance to their cause and their departed king. The arrival of great numbers of elegant and beribboned men and women was a strong influence on Virginian dress and manners."[19] Cromwell's forces, conversely, expressed the Puritan religious doctrine by adopting a much simpler, more modest mode of dress: muted colors, minimal pleats and laces, and very little embellishment. Once the Roundheads won the war, this plain costume tended to prevail in England at least until the Restoration in 1660. Although there were other Protestant sects that had similar ideas about self-fashioning, the term *puritan* has become synonymous with this trend toward simplicity.

In the decades leading up to the start of the English civil war, many Puritans were departing England to create communities where they could practice their religion without the threat of persecution. They brought with them the sartorial conventions of Puritan England. In the 1630s, the General Court, the governing body of the

MBC, passed a series of sumptuary laws—laws restricting what clothing people could wear, sometimes making distinctions by class or profession; these laws now provide a detailed record of what luxuries Puritans found objectionable. The first such law, passed in 1634, prohibited residents from flaunting "new fashions, or long hair, or anything of the like nature." In 1639, the General Court banned lace for commoners and forbade short sleeves. Of course, the need for those prohibitions suggests that people living in the colony were attracted to such embellishments.[20]

Despite the twenty-year conflict between Cromwell's parliamentarians and the monarchy, the governing families of settlements in seventeenth-century New England always considered themselves English, even while the place of their religion in England seemed at risk. As they removed themselves geographically from the center of British power, they wished to remain British subjects and held out hope that a change in government at home would bring the prevailing religious values in England into accord with their own.

That dedication to Britain was different from the experience of their descendants, literal and otherwise, who over a century later made the difficult determination that they would no longer be subjects of the British Crown and, thus, instigated the American Revolution. In the intervening years, however, colonial New Englanders were mostly unequivocal in their British American identity and tended to follow, more or less closely, English and European fashion trends—with a dash of Puritan sensibility thrown in for good measure.

FIG I.12: Increase Mather, by John van der Spriett, 1688, sporting a Very Puritan Style.

Colonial Bostonians were inspired by European tastes in all of their decorative arts, including architecture and home furnishings. During the late seventeenth and early eighteenth centuries, as global trade expanded and new materials became less expensive and more accessible in the British market, so too did ideas and aesthetics. When certain trends swept across Europe, they also swept across the ocean and took hold in English America. Were Asian-derived motifs of flora and fauna transforming the decorative arts in England? Then they were sure to ripple through New England homes and wardrobes as well. As sinuous vines, leaves, and polychrome flowers became nearly ubiquitous in English dress, Americans would seek to acquire or create the same ornament for themselves. One excellent example of this iconography can be seen in the hand-embroidered wedding dress and petticoat of Elizabeth Bull Price, garments that she wore for her 1735 Boston wedding.[21] At roughly the same time, Mary Woodbury of Beverly, Massachusetts, embroidered a baptismal apron with vining flowers, urns, and flying birds of paradise, drawing on the influence of Eastern design elements.

above, FIG I.13: Detail of embroidery by Mary Woodbury. See Fig. 1.7.

ght, FIG I.14: Detail of embroidery by Elizabeth Bull Price, courtesy Revolutionary Spaces. See Fig. 1.8.

The connection to global markets, and especially the dependence on British trade, would take on a very different meaning in the years leading up to the Declaration of Independence in 1776. In the 1760s, the British government began to aggravate its American subjects with the imposition of a series of import tariffs, specifically the Sugar Act and the Stamp Act, both 1764–1765, and three years later the Townshend Acts, which imposed duties on a broad range of items. The latter prompted an effort in the colonies to purchase fewer imported goods and increase domestic production, which escalated to formal boycotts by consumers and non-importation agreements among merchants. While the effectiveness of these calls to action was limited, it did become a badge of honor among New Englanders to clothe themselves in "homespun" fabric, eschewing the styles and luxuries most obviously derived from English trade.

The pushback from the colonies did motivate Parliament to dismantle most of the Towshend Acts in 1770, excepting the duty on tea. That tariff became increasingly burdensome in subsequent years, culminating in the Boston Tea Party on December 16, 1773, which in turn prompted the authorities in England to respond with an aggressive suite of new laws known collectively as the Coercive Acts. With these, Parliament sought to punish the colonies economically and politically—especially Massachusetts, where the Port of Boston was closed and the colony's self-governance was restricted. These measures backfired, as the colonies came together to break from the British Empire and create a new nation.

Of course, the move to independence was not without its own challenges for Americans. The Revolutionary War, starting in 1775, disrupted transatlantic trade to American ports, amplifying the need for domestic production that had begun with the ideological resistance to British goods. Furthermore, just as the break from the empire created dire shortages in the former colonies, it also entailed instability in the currency system, which the Continental Congress and the provincial legislatures attempted to manage. The Massachusetts General Assembly, for example, addressed price fluctuations, including rampant inflation, by setting fixed prices for goods and labor, as did New York and other New England states.[22]

A snapshot of these efforts in 1777 gives a sense of the relative value that the government considered reasonable, albeit expressed in pounds and shillings, twenty of which made up a pound. As a baseline, consider the prices set by the New Hampshire General Assembly for 1777 for food and drink: meals at taverns were not to exceed one shilling apiece, and the prices stipulated for a gallon of rum were three shillings ten pence for the New England spirit and six shillings eight pence for the same from the West Indies (twelve pence made up a shilling). Income for a tailor's labor, per day, was held at three shillings, and a carpenter's, at four shillings. In New Hampshire, the daily pay for a farm hand was three shillings six pence, and the value of "Woman's common work" was set at two shillings six pence per week. The declared prices for clothing in New Hampshire included footwear—men's shoes, nine shillings; women's, seven shillings; and "half boots, best," thirteen shillings six pence.[23] The cost of making a full woolen suit could not exceed one pound four shillings, and anyone seeking to purchase the "Best dressed wool cloth, ¾ yard wide" would expect to pay nine shillings.

Throughout the seventeenth and eighteenth centuries, and even into the nineteenth century, the purchase price for an article of new clothing—especially at the higher end—was substantial enough that each piece constituted an investment. Even as new styles made older garments unfashionable, they held their value as useful commodities. Consequently, many items were assiduously maintained within a family, sometimes altered for new uses or restyled to match new trends.

The archival sources that remain today—the written and the woven—speak to how well New Englanders reused and reinvented their clothes. Many of the items illustrated on these pages can testify to generations of alteration. Jackets, waistcoats, petticoats, and gowns were worked to match new styles and to flatter new figures. Cloth retained from a well-worn garment could be cut down to become something entirely different, sometimes even transformed into shoes.[24] Examples of such repaired, reused, and refashioned clothing are found in many museum collections and mentioned in countless daybooks.

While some textiles became family souvenirs from sentimental attachment, clothing and textiles also held real value akin to cash. As clothing passed from generation to generation, seventeenth- and eighteenth-century wills and probate inventories sometimes recorded a monetary value for each item, including these among all of the other household property of the deceased. When Sarah Williams, the twenty-year-old daughter of a wealthy family in western Massachusetts, passed away in 1738, her executors inventoried her treasury of high-end attire.[25] The extensive list includes, among other

FIG I.15: In the 19th century, Bostonians enjoyed parties that referenced costumes of earlier eras. While most of the individuals in this 1888 photograph adopted attire reminiscent of Renaissance Europe, Amy Heard Grey—on the far right—chose an 18th-century style, including the shoes and a quilted petticoat. Outfits like this could have been adapted from clothing actually passed down within a family.

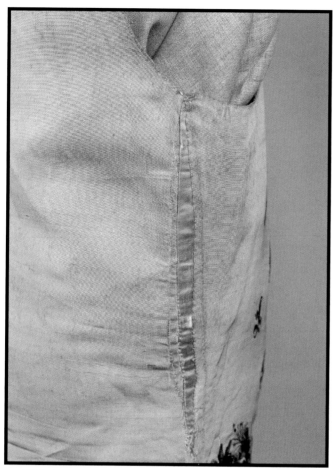

FIG I.9b: Detail, William Tailer's waistocat altered for expanded girth.

items, a taffeta robe valued at six pounds; a damask robe, at three pounds fifteen shillings; one chintz and one calico robe; and cloth cut for a riding habit and trimming, as well as other references to unfinished garments and accessories. When older individuals composed wills, as a family matriarch or patriarch usually did, they might stipulate recipients for specific garments, bequeathing them as valuable goods to younger family members or domestic staff.[26]

The real value of a recently deceased family member's wardrobe could be recuperated through auctions, which did a lively trade in sec-

ondhand clothing in England and America.[27] In 1726, an advertisement for clothes from a gentleman's estate appeared in the July 18 issue of the *Boston Gazette*:

> On Thursday next the 21st Currant at 6 of the Clock in the Afternoon, at the Sun Tavern on Dock Square, will be Sold to the Highest Bidder, Sundry Waring Apparel New, which belong'd to a Gentleman Deceased. Also Sundry new Suits of Cloaths, a Box of Fine Caster Hats, a Parcel of Silk Stockings, also some Worsted Ditto, and sundry other sorts of Goods.

Through such auctions, as well as other retail systems, the secondhand clothing market was a thriving business, distributing goods for a buyer's personal use or to repurpose and possibly resell.

The trade also provided an income stream for many merchants, as demonstrated in the 1747 book *The London Tradesman*: "The Salesmen deal in Old Cloaths, and sometimes in New. They trade very largely, and some of them are worth some Thousands: They are mostly Taylors, at least, must have a perfect Skill in that Craft."[28] Beverly Lemire has noted that a colonial demand for low-cost clothing was also met through imports of outdated items, often arriving from England in bulk shipments identified as "Wearing Apparel." It was not unusual for the cheapest of such goods to be acquired to clothe servants and especially enslaved people laboring on plantations.[29] While not technically "used," the garments sold this way did not carry the price of new clothing because they were typically out of date and had lost so much market value that they were, in essence, "remaindered" for quick sale at lower prices.

The trade in cheap, used, or outdated goods helps bring to light the many Americans who did not have the ability either to own high-quality new attire or to save any fabric as a remembrance. For many families, every remnant of any textile could serve for barter and trade. Middling and poor households would put aside bits and bobs for possible trade or for cash at a future time, as John Styles has shown in his research. These savings, as it were, constituted assets that could help during hard times.[30]

For individuals seeking to escape either enslavement or servitude more generally, clothing was a vital asset, as it could serve as a disguise or as currency. Concrete details about fashion and how clothing was used for transactions, both social and economic, appear in the thousands of "runaway" advertisements published in early American newspapers. Textiles were also often among the extra items a fleeing person, indentured or enslaved, might choose to carry with them. A traveler could benefit from the layers, depending on the weather, and also from the opportunity to sell or trade pieces en route. For example, a 1716 *Boston Newsletter* notice alerted readers that the subject, an "Indian Man named Nim," "wears a Hat, Shoes, Stockings," but it also reported his doubled garments: "two new shirts, a new waistcoat, and breeches of white course linen, and the same blew striped," as well as "a homespun Coat."[31]

While Nim's breeches and coat may have been his usual attire for everyday work, many descriptions were very precise about finery that the individual may have carried away for trading—or perhaps in a quest for self-reinvention. Certainly the "green velvet waistcoat with silver buttons" that Solomon Haynes took with him in 1768 could have served either purpose.[32] Noting that Haynes had also "carried with him . . . many other kinds of clothes," enslaver James Scrosby likely knew the value of the textiles,

adding it mentally to the sum of his "property" loss in the form of the person whom he had held in bondage. For the individual embarking on the hazardous path to freedom, however, such garments constituted a substantial and long-term financial resource—and possibly a modicum of recompense for the labor and self-determination already stolen from them.

For Nicholas Classon, a white servant, some very fine apparel in his 1728 traveling wardrobe may have provided the costume he needed to lift himself up to an improved social and economic echelon. Erstwhile an apprentice in the printing shop of Philadelphia publisher Andrew Bradford, Classon escaped wearing "a gray Drugget Coat lin'd and trim'd with Black, a white Demity Jacket, also a white Fustin Coat with Mettle Buttons, and faced in the Neck with red Velvit, a Pair of Leather Breeches, and a Pair of striped Linnen home-spun Breeches." He also had with him "a short bob Wigg."[33] Possibly heading for Boston—or so Bradford suspected when he posted the runaway advertisement in the *Boston Gazette*—Classon might just succeed in his escape and achieve a higher station in a new city, presenting himself as an independent freeman with the right clothes.

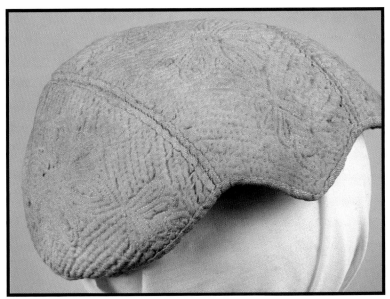

THE SARTORIAL COLONIAL WOMAN

AMONG THE seventeenth-century textiles preserved in the collections of the Massachusetts Historical Society is a small piece of cloth, barely four inches square, that belonged to Priscilla Mullins Alden (ca. 1602–ca. 1685), the *Mayflower* passenger immortalized by the stories of her courtship with and subsequent marriage to fellow passenger John Alden, the ship's cooper. This fragment, a souvenir that has been passed down in the family for generations, conveys some information about itself that can provide insight into the material culture of the transatlantic world in the seventeenth century.[1] The yarn has been identified as wool from northern Europe and woven from separate skeins. The particular green-blue hue of the fragment was a popular color in both the seventeenth and eighteenth centuries, but the original color may have been quite different, changing with exposure to light and other environmental conditions.[2] Because the pattern created by the weaving is visible on both sides of the cloth, it is known as *damask*, and one side would have exhibited a slightly glossy surface when new. Possibly Priscilla Mullins brought this garment with her when she and her family set out on the *Mayflower* in 1620, though it could also have been shipped to her later. Even with the evidence intrinsic to this item, a great deal remains unknown. Who saved it? When? And from what item of clothing was it spared?

The answer to the last question, at least, has only three options, as the constitutive elements of Western women's public attire remained quite constant for centuries and over many continents. Although the terminology varied depending on time and place, the three primary components

persisted and are still familiar to us today, albeit sometimes with unfamiliar names: a garment to cover the legs, often called a *petticoat* and meant to be seen in whole or in part—but decidedly not an undergarment; a garment to cover the torso, such as a shirtwaist or bodice and sometimes encompassing very specific forms such as the stomacher or jacket; and one long piece to pull it together, historically invoked by familiar terms such as *gown*, *robe*, and *dress*, but also commonly called a *mantua* in the eighteenth century. There were undergarments as well, including typically a chemise and stays, a bodice, or a corset. Layers of underpetticoats were donned in cold temperatures, along with heavy knit stockings.

Like the terminology naming these articles of clothing, many other conventions of Western women's costume shifted depending on the era and region, as well as the status of the wearer. The overall shape, or silhouette, effected by the complete trio of garments morphed from decade to decade. While the essential components remained the same for the clothing worn every day by women of different socio-economic strata, the quality of the textiles used and the dressmaking itself varied widely. Cloth and color would change depending on technology and trade routes, which would also affect what was perceived as most desirable. In the seventeenth and eighteenth centuries, the most elaborate and expensive ensembles would have been for presentation at court, formal functions at royal courts in cities like London, Paris, and Versailles. Since those styles set the look of power, they were also echoed, in less extravagant form, in women's everyday dress, especially among the elite classes. In America, thousands of miles from court culture, self-presentation played a less prominent, but still important, role.

Although we do not know which item of clothing gave rise to Priscilla Alden's now four-hundred-year-old bit of fabric, we can surmise from her biography that she would not have had occasion to wear presentation attire. The Mullins party (comprising Priscilla; her parents, Wil-

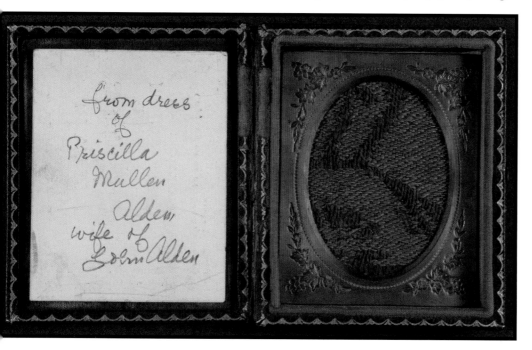

Preceding pages:
FIG 1.1a: Leverett petticoat, tracing detail.
FIG 1.2a: Priscilla Mullins Alden, dress fragment, unframed.

This page, FIG 1.2b: Alden dress fragment, framed.

Following pages:
FIG 1.1b: Tracing by Alice Scott Brown Knight Smith.

liam and Alice; her younger brother, Joseph; and a servant or possible apprentice, Robert) hailed from Dorking, in Surrey, where William was a successful shoemaker, commonly referred to at that time as a *cordwainer*. The Mullinses did not emigrate as dissenters, seeking religious freedom, but instead traveled as "Strangers" aboard the ship—people who invested in the colony as a financial endeavor and were perhaps looking for opportunities for acquiring land and business in the new world. On their journey in 1620, William brought with him extensive stock for his trade, including leather and completed shoes and boots, knowing that these goods and his skill would be valuable resources in the nascent settlement.[3] With no regional shoemaking industry—or even established colonial systems for treating the raw materials—the area all but guaranteed a high demand for his product.

A decade earlier, the first shoemakers had arrived in Jamestown, the Virginia settlement, and within six years the shoe trade there was thriving.[4] Capt. John Smith gave vivid testimony of the harm the Virginia colonists endured "for want of Shooes": "among the Oyster Banks wee tore our hatts and Clothes and those being worne, wee tied the Barkes of trees about our Feete to keepe them from being Cutt by the shelles amongst which we must goe or starve"—a warning he followed by noting "yett how many thousand of Shooes hath been transported to these plantations."[5] Further suggesting the rate at which the English settlers went through their footwear as they traveled on foot in unfamiliar terrain, Smith provided a list of "such necessaries" to help potential émigrés know "better how to provide for themselves." In contrast to his recommendation of one cap and one waistcoat, Smith urged each man to bring "4 paire of shooes." William Wood, of the Massachusetts

Bay Colony, founded in Boston north of and a decade later than the Plymouth community, made similar recommendations: "Every man likewise must carry over good store of Apparrell. . . . Hats, Bootes, Shooes, good Irish stockings, which if they be good, are much more serviceable than knit-ones [from England]."[6] As settlements took hold along the eastern seaboard, the demand for shoes generated local providers. North of Boston, cordwainer Philip Kirkland (or Kertland) initiated a trade that would eventually confer the title of Shoe City on his town, Lynn, Massachusetts.[7] Clearly, the Mullins family was making a fair bet with the move to the American colonies.

While ultimately we know little about Priscilla's time in Plymouth prior to her circa 1622/1623 marriage to John Alden, we can surmise that, in addition to the dress represented by this fragment, she arrived with very good shoes, probably of the latest style and certainly with several pairs. Sadly, the rest of the Mullins household died within months of landing, leaving Priscilla without family in a new land. But the young woman had at her disposal a fairly substantial inheritance. Priscilla would have inherited land and livestock as well as clothing (including her mother's), domestic goods, and her father's shoemaking tools and materials. These last items, along with his stock of finished shoes and boots, would have held considerable value in this time of scarcity.[8] It is tempting to speculate that the dress from which the damask fragment comes made up a part of that inheritance, or even that Priscilla wore it while being courted by John Alden. Having crossed the ocean as the ship's cooper, John was slated to return to England in April 1621, but he did not do so, perhaps due to a burgeoning interest in his fellow émigrée.

Some fifteen years in Priscilla Alden's wake, Hannah Hudson (1621–1643 or 1646) emigrated with her parents from Kingston-on-Hull in Yorkshire in 1635, arriving at the Massachusetts Bay Colony; four years later, she married John Leverett (1616–1679).[9] Like Priscilla's elusive woven wool souvenir, a few tantalizing records remain of a petticoat attributed to Hannah's wardrobe by family memory; these records— a tracing on muslin and a note—have made it possible to imagine what the original may have looked like. The tracing was donated to the Massachusetts Historical Society in 1953 by Alice (Scott) Brown Knight Smith, the widow of one of John and Hannah's direct descendants. In the accompanying note, Smith described the original fabric, as well as the look and feel of the garment: she wrote that it "was of blue gros-grain silk quilted in white silk thread and had the effect of pale silver tissue."[10]

Both the fabric mentioned here and the quilting represented in Smith's tracing speak to the broad range of functions petticoats served, from basic utility to rich and complex social communication. A petticoat would be quilted to provide warmth, with two layers of fabric sewn together and stuffed with cotton or wool batting, which made them a particular favorite in the northern colonies. But such utility did not preclude an ornamental purpose: as with this item, the needlework for the quilting could create all manner of artful images and patterns that would have been visible to people around the wearer. Based on the textile that Alice Smith ascribed to the original, it must have been an elegant garment. Having the "effect of pale silver tissue" identifies it as a particularly expensive piece, since in the seventeenth century, the word *tissue* referred to a silk fabric woven with silver metallic threads, which made the garment shine and glint.

The Leverett petticoat had survived in the family for hundreds of years before it was destroyed in the San Francisco earthquake of 1906. Fortunately, ten years earlier Smith had copied the figures of the quilting using a method called "pricking" because of the way the stitching was pricked into paper. After 1906, she used that paper to make another copy of the entire petticoat, this one drawn to scale with pencil on muslin. That tracing—Smith's gift to the MHS—shows the figures that were quilted into the fabric and thus gives us a vivid illustration of a petticoat believed to have been worn in seventeenth-century New England.

Alice Smith's note also informs us that, according to family tradition, John Leverett had brought the garment "as a gift to his wife from Holland"—which would also date it between 1639, when they married, and circa 1645. Even as a young man, Hannah's bridegroom was close to the governing class in Puritan Boston. John Leverett was the only son of Thomas Leverett, a man who held prominent roles in Boston's religious and civic leadership. By the time of his marriage to Hannah, John was just at the outset of what would be his illustrious career; as yet, he had only served the colony in military capacities and possibly embarked on some merchant ventures, the latter speculation strengthened by the family's belief that he brought the petticoat from Holland. Within five years of his marriage to Hannah, he would be in England commanding troops for Oliver Cromwell, the leader of the parliamentarian fight against the royalist forces that sought to return a Stuart king, Charles I or his son Charles II, to power. John would continue on, after Hannah's death, to undertake further military and diplomatic missions for Cromwell and the MBC, and he would rise through the ranks of Boston politics, becoming governor in

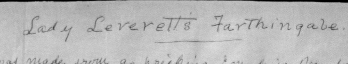

Lady Leverett's Farthingale.

This tracing of Lady Leverett's farthingale was made from a pricking I made in December 1896 the farthingale was destroyed in the fire and earthquake of 1906 in San Francisco. Sir John Leverett, Colonial Governor of Massachusetts from 1673 to 1676 brought the farthingale as a gift to his wife from Holland. The farthingale was of blue gros-grain silk quilted in white silk thread and had the effect of pale silver tissue. It descended on the "distaff side" in my first-husband's family. I have drawn this on muslin to preserve it December 1953 in my 87th year.

the 1670s.[11] Although much of that arc was still in his future when Hannah passed away, as a young man he was already well esteemed and well connected in the colonies and across the Atlantic.

What we know about John Leverett's life provides a great deal of context for the petticoat, particularly as a reminder of the vibrancy of the Atlantic economy even in the first half of the seventeenth century. It also presents a useful counterpoint to the utilitarian demand for shoes illustrated by the Mullins family, demonstrating in contrast the presence of luxury textiles in Boston a little more than a decade after its settlement. Petticoats had a role in the social power of luxury during the seventeenth and eighteenth centuries, when women often intended their petticoats to be seen.[12] Those who could chose arresting textiles like bright silks, maybe even sparkling brocaded silks, or the quilted glazed wool known as calamanco, that would peek out from open robes or pair with a short jacket similarly fashioned. As a deliberately visible garment, the petticoat provided a canvas for signaling the wearer's social status and especially her family's wealth.

In both England and colonial America, many women with the means would invest in petticoats made of luxurious and costly imported fabrics and colored with those dyes that were most difficult to obtain. As for the item John Leverett bought for his wife, a Dutch silk petticoat would not have been out of place among the seventeenth-century merchant elite of Boston—not even among the Puritan merchant elite. Indeed, adding such a fashionable garment to the Leverett wardrobe, transported from the Netherlands as a gift, would have confirmed John's status as a scion of a leading family.

Gaps in the information we have about this garment, however, still leave some doubt about its exact date of origin. Although we can state with some confidence that a petticoat for Hannah was purchased around 1640, we cannot know what alterations it went through in the centuries between that time and the pricking that Alice Smith made, nor can we know for sure that the petticoat Smith's husband inherited hadn't come from a later generation of the Leverett family. One of the key complexities this garment presents is the quilting, since the earliest extant petticoats with this kind of figuring date from around the 1730s, almost a hundred years after Hannah's death.

The strongest evidence for the style of quilted pattern depicted in the pricking of the Leverett petticoat appears in the mid eighteenth century, further supporting a later date of creation than the initial family account suggests.[13] The original owner of the petticoat Alice Smith traced may have been Abigail Buttolph (1704–1776), who wed Hannah's great-grandson, Knight Leverett, in Boston in 1726, and family legend simply created a more storied past for it. Even so, it's very likely that the petticoat represented by Smith's muslin tracing had been modified considerably from the size and shape of the original. Valuable garments were frequently altered to adapt them to suit changing fashions or even to create entirely new articles of clothing from the materials. And the preferred style, including shape and length, for petticoats morphed frequently across the centuries, changing along with the prevailing notion of the ideal feminine silhouette.

Each shift in women's fashion instigated, and depended on, changes in the shape of the petticoat and its substructure of hoops, also sometimes called *baskets* or *panniers*, which were made from raw materials including cane; wood, such as willow; or baleen, which is often called *whalebone* but is actually a type of pliable bristle found in whale mouths. These supports were an essen-

Fashioning
the New England Family

As America's first historical society, we have collected family papers since 1791. Lovingly preserved textiles that accompanied these documents speak eloquently to the pride and respect held by the family members who treasured and saved these objects for later generations. Yet once received in our collections, preservation concerns dictated their removal to separate storage. Divorced from that familial connection, through the years these textiles have been considered merely pretty, or interesting relics of a bygone age, largely unexamined and rarely displayed.

All of the early textiles in our holdings come from Boston's elite families. Because textiles were so valuable in the 17th and 18th centuries, they were often bequeathed from generation to generation along with silver and land. Accordingly, most of the examples that survive today are of the finest kind. The importance of these luxury goods as political and social statements carried through the colonial period and beyond. By the end of the 19th century the availability of specialized garments and accessories through a wider range of sources meant that people at more levels of society could indulge their sartorial taste.

In recent years the concept of examining textiles and clothing as primary historical sources has proved richly rewarding and continues to provide context for how we understand our past. In preparation for this exhibition, we have learned that even the wealthiest families repaired, refashioned, and passed along their clothing. Each item provides a wealth of information when we find the right questions to ask. Well versed in deciphering manuscripts here at the Massachusetts Historical Society, we are just beginning to read the stories that make up our textiles and we are delighted to welcome you as we begin this journey.

Above, FIG 1.3: Temperence Pickering petticoat, on loan from the University of New Hampshire for display at the MHS. This quilted petticoat belonged to Temperance Pickering (1730-1823) of Newington, N.H. Exemplary of such garments in the mid 18th century, this petticoat has an outer layer of yellow silk quilted to a lining of yellow and white checked wool with an interlining of flax.

Left, FIG. 1.4: Leverett petticoat, re-constructed by milliners from Colonial Williamsburg, on display at the MHS.

tial part of life for fashionable women, at both formal functions and even relatively informal public engagements. Like the quality of fabric or dye or the degree of embellishment, how well a woman's attire achieved the desired figure of her era signaled her status.

At the close of the seventeenth century, the dominant silhouette was a relatively modest bell shape supported by rounded hoops. As the eighteenth century unfurled, that form contracted in some parts of the figure and billowed out in others, combining at points the extreme of a "wasp waist" with a skirt so broad it might be three times the wearer's width. The hoops for that petticoat necessarily became quite large and built out over the hips. Hip pads and bum rolls became common additions to undergarments in the latter half of the century, giving a new roundness to the petticoat and, by the end of the century, an emphasis specifically on the rear. The expected shape varied not just by era but also depending on region and purpose, the most rigid and extreme being reserved for attendance at royal court functions.[14]

A roughly standard terminology for the different styles, as effected by the arrangement of skirt, bodice, and robe, emerged over the decades as well. One of the earliest, and most common, was *mantua*, which in the late seventeenth century denoted a type of loose gown worn open in the front to show the petticoat, usually creating a relatively relaxed but full silhouette—something fairly user-friendly for everyday wear and possibly a corrective to the very structured type of formal attire that had taken hold in the sixteenth-century Spanish court and migrated to French royal functions thereafter. Later in the eighteenth century, *mantua* more often described a robe worn over stays, a stomacher, and a coordinating petticoat; the garment

had become, like other styles in the eighteenth century, more shaped, with the waist more defined. However, the term eventually became so generalized that it could refer both to that loose and informal starting point and to a very luxurious item donned to make an impression at formal affairs. In fact it came to serve as the parent word for the various offshoots of the robe-over-petticoat ensemble, including those that follow. The term *mantua maker* also became a common synonym for *dressmaker*, persisting into the nineteenth century.

The main descendants of the early mantua in the eighteenth century were the *robe à l'anglaise* and *robe à la française*, also known as a *sack-back* dress in reference to the pleats gathered at the back of the neckline. In contrast, the *robe à l'anglaise*—a favorite of both British and British American women by the mid-eighteenth century—had a well-fitted back. The prized examples of this garment featured superb pattern matching, frequently of elegant and expensive silks.

In the earlier part of the century, however, the *robe à la française* was a dominant style. The deep box pleats that distinguished it—what we know today as "Watteau" pleats, after the painter who frequently depicted them—cascaded gracefully down from the back of the neckline. There, the fabric flowed loosely away from the body, and the bottom of the skirt was often much larger in circumference than were the shoulders. Initially an informal, loose-fitting garment, it became increasingly formal over the course of the eighteenth century and its silhouette became more pronounced. In the course of this evolution, the skirts became boxy—even distinctly rectangular in the most extreme instances—and very broad from side to side but with a close-fitting front and back. This created an expansive swath of textile that acted like a canvas on which all manner of precious materials were on display: complex quilting patterns, luxurious materials such as gold and silver threads, spangles, and silk damasks and brocades in complex weaves. The close-fitting bodice, by contrast, diminished in breadth from shoulders to waist, which could be quite pinched.

The most iconic feature of this style, the extreme emphasis on the hips, was accomplished through the engineering of side hoops, typically made of baleen or bent wood. For the creation of this type of garment, but for others as well, skilled mantua makers draped swaths of textiles around customers for a first fitting. Each *robe à la française* thus occasioned an extravagant use of material to create the pleats and especially the petticoats, which required excessive yardage of costly textiles for coverage. Hence, the wider the petticoat, the more expensive the garment became.

Mantua makers were a necessity for any aristocratic English woman who attended royal

FIG 1.5: *Portrait of Lady Juliana Penn*, portrait by Arthur Devis.
Oil on canvas, 1752. Made in England, Europe. Philadelphia Museum of Art: 125th Anniversary Acquisition. Gift of Susanne Strassburger Anderson, Valerie Anderson Story, and Veronica Anderson Macdonald from the estate of Mae Bourne and Ralph Beaver Strassburger, 2004. Accession 2004-201-2.

functions. From that first fitting, through cutting and sewing a gown, to the final fitting and tweaks, a mantua maker made sure that a lady was appropriately clad for her public appearances. Such dressmakers were also a part of the colonial world. Since even elite American women did not typically travel overseas before the nineteenth century, their access to prevailing fashions in England depended on imports or domestically made imitations. Production of the latter was aided by periodicals and printed memorandum books that included patterns or engravings of the latest styles. Regarding petticoats specifically, although American women often made their own, the evidence suggests that those who could afford to purchase one were likely to do so for reasons of cost or expediency. And a great many petticoats were exported from Great Britain to the colonies.[15] American women engaged in the same fashion choices as their British cousins, even embracing the extravagant hoop petticoat, although American taste generally toned down the extremely unwieldy dimensions associated with London and life at court.

Nonetheless, American women who had the means could demonstrate their wealth and status with the extravagant use of fabric and embellishments—the very definition of luxury. Indeed, luxury was to some degree the inverse relationship between the cost of creating an item and its utility. Gloves, for example, had long been a symbol of wealth and social position because they signified that the wearer did not engage in any manual labor. The sheer lack of functionality and the impracticality of delicate laced gloves or supple white kidskin leather made them accessories to covet. A luxury item was a status symbol precisely because it demonstrated one's ability to expend wealth on useless things, such

as gloves and an abundance of expensive textiles used for one garment.

This kind of display also became a target for critics in England and in America—typically male "wits" who critiqued this taste for excess as a particularly feminine fault. The circulation of these opinions from the British Isles to America appears in many periodicals, such as this 1754 printing of "A Satire on Women's Dress" in the *Boston Evening Post*, which had appeared in at least a few British papers in 1753. The poem provides a compendium of fashion trends, small and large, enticing to female consumers:

> Let your gown be a Sack, blue, yellow or
>   green,
> and frizzle your elbows with ruffles
> furl off your lawn aprons with flounces in rows
> puff and pucker up knots on your arms and
>   your toes
> make your petticoat short that a hoop eight
>   yards wide
> may decently show how your garters are tyed
> with fringes of knoting.[16]

The yardage of extra material required to cover panniers—"a hoop eight yards wide"—became a particular object of admiration and disdain in the eighteenth century. In England, well-known satirists such as Jonathan Swift, Joseph Addison, and Richard Steele published comical screeds on the immodesty and proportions of fashionable skirts in popular English periodicals like the *Spectator* and the *Tatler*. For example, in 1710 Addison put the hooped petticoat on mock trial, deeming it too large to gain admittance to his house.[17] Artists like Thomas Rowlandson, whose prints were frequently reproduced in periodicals as well, also satirized what many considered the folly of women's dress.[18]

The expression and consumption of these opinions were not reserved to England. Copies of the *Tatler* could be found in colonial American libraries, and Bostonians voiced similar horrors—often in similarly colorful terms. In the summer of 1722, young Benjamin Franklin deployed his fictional persona Silence Dogood in the *New-England Courant* to draw the absurdity of the hoop petticoat—and to do so with reference specifically to Boston's landscape: "These monstrous topsy-turvy *Mortar-Pieces* are neither fit for the Church, the Hall, or the Kitchen; and if a Number of them were well mounted on *Noddles-Island*, they would look more like Engines of War for bombarding the Town, than Ornaments of the Fair Sex."[19] Two months later, another complainant to the *Courant* lambasted "the scandalous and Monstrous Fashion of hoop petticoats." Loading them with further epithets such as "Immodest and obscene," "odious and Criminal," and "unseemly and immodest," the writer captured more fully the affront to public modesty in the street and in church:

> And I am sure it is neither comfortable or convenient especially in the winter or in high Winds, when every ruffling blast is apt to lift them up, and expose their uncomely Parts to every one's view. . . . Neither are they decent or convenient in the Church, unless every one might have a large Pew to themselves: I my self, last Sunday, saw one of them tilted up in a Pew, by the jostling of a Boy, and whelm'd over the top of a Chair, which was not unloos'd without some Blushes and Confusion.[20]

Two years later, another letter to the *Courant* recounted the difficulty of navigating a public street when large hoop petticoats dominated the sidewalks: "And as I was mustering my Intellectual Forces, I discovered a Fleet of Hoop Petticoats bearing down upon me; and though I was resolute to stand the Smartest Attack, I soon found the Surges of a tempestuous Tittle-tattle run too high for me to ride with any safety in so boisterous a Region."[21]

Of course, in their very sense of urgency, these critics recognized the powerful appeal of the fashion for outsized petticoats, remarking as the August 1722 *Courant* writer does that "admirers of these loathsome Go-Carts may perhaps plead that they are beautiful and ornamental." This author also noted how strongly the appeal of the hoop petticoat, "worn by all our females (from the best lady to the poorest kitchen wench)," cut across social position. Franklin's piece also

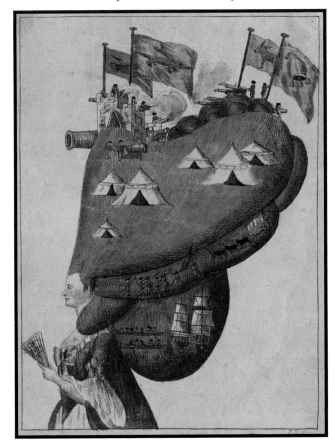

FIG 1.6: *Noddle-Island; or, How Are We Decieved*. This 1776 cartoon by London printmakers Mary and Matthew Darly lampoons both excess in women's styles and the failure of British forces at Bunker Hill.

insinuated the leveling effect of petticoat aspiration by arguing its unfitness for "the Church, the Hall, or the Kitchen."

Despite the popularity of this kind of lampooning, the range of choices that women made about their clothing all had valuable functions, many utilitarian but all with some degree of social meaning. The decision to wear certain garments or textiles divulged much about women's roles in early American society, their patterns of consumption and trade, their agency and self-fashioning, their politics, their economic situations, and their opportunities for education. And while even the wealthiest women of Boston were barred from the centers of power—the General Court, the Governor's Council—they had authority at many social events and shared information where they met and conversed at fashionable shops. Some of those shops were run by women, among them Henrietta Caine, Elizabeth Murray, Jane Gillam, and Elizabeth Renken.[22]

Colonial women also shared responsibility for maintaining the clothes for their household, and most women's garments were made locally and sewn at home. Consequently, certain tasks related to needlework occupied many women for much of their lives. Mainly, the work fell into two categories. The first comprised those tasks essential to the care of clothing, such as mending, darning, altering for fashion or weight change, and remaking for a new purpose or owner. The second category encompassed non-essential items and decorative work, such as making accessories and display items—pocketbooks, watch strings, sewing cases, samplers—and embellishing all manner of garments and accessories with embroidery. Depending on a woman's socio-economic position, she would likely spend more time working in one category than the other. Both required at least a basic competence

with a needle—and some specialties demanded advanced expertise.[23]

Needlework of the ornamental variety was thus a key index of a young woman's accomplishment and her social status. "Far from being mere useless frivolities, as castigated by critics," argues historian Susan Schoelwer, "needlework performed important cultural work. Like other physical signs of gentility—symmetrical Georgian-style houses, elegantly written letters, correct posture—decorative needlework signaled refinement."[24] Schoelwer also explains how education figured into this equation: "The fact that families were willing to incur the costs for these schools urges a reconsideration of the cultural significance and meaning of female accomplishments—needlework chief among them."

In the eighteenth century, schools imparting these accomplishments existed in major cities along the eastern seaboard, including Philadelphia, New York, Boston, Hartford, Newport, and Charleston. In these establishments, students learned the "gentle arts" of needlework, painting, French, and dance, among other skills. In a Philadelphia paper in 1723, one school offered the services of "one Mrs. Rodes" to teach "Young Ladies or Gentlewomen" to draw "all manner of Patterns for flourishing on Muslin and those in fashion of Lace, which is very pretty and quickly learned. She likewise draws Patterns for Embroidering of petticoats etc."[25] In New England, many such "female academies" existed, and in Boston dozens of women taught embroidery, lace-making, and whitework (white thread embroidery on a white ground, such as linen or muslin), among other specialties. Advertising in the *Boston Gazette and Country Journal* in 1766, Mary Phillips offered to "teach young Ladies to sew at Three Shillings per week, and Marking, Irish and Ten[t] Stitch, and Embroidering." Typi-

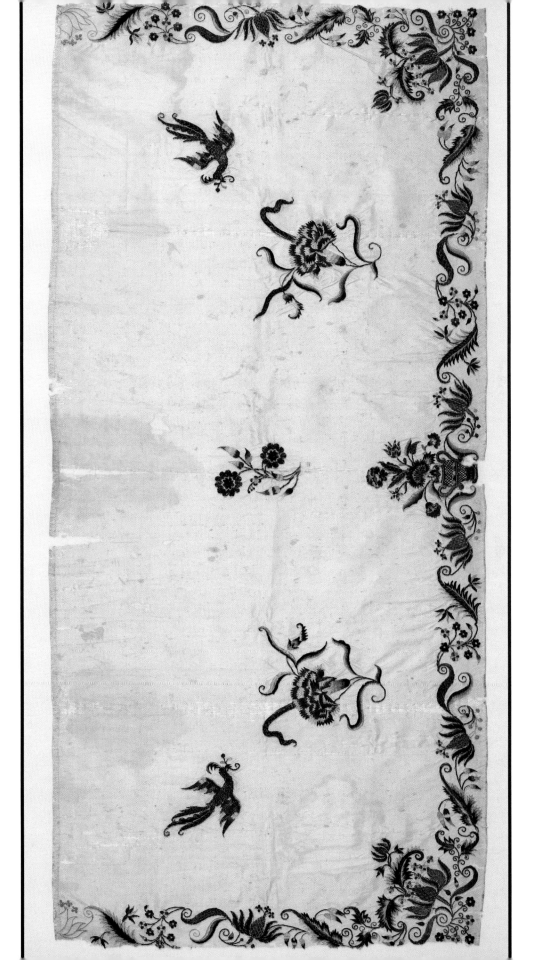

FIG 1.7: Mary
Woodbury apron.
See also Fig. I.13.

cally known by the name of the proprietress, similar Boston schools were run by "Miss Perkins" and "Mrs. Rowson."[26]

The value that this kind of ornamental needlework could hold within a family is apparent from how many have survived and are now preserved in museum collections, which document the quantity and variety that women created. Two early eighteenth-century examples from the Boston area show the level of expertise, and the dedication, that went into preparing garments for prominent social events: a baptismal apron by Mary Woodbury (1717–1748) of Beverly and a wedding dress by Elizabeth Bull (1717–1780) of Boston.

Woodbury's apron is a length of white silk, lavishly embroidered along the sides and bottom in polychrome silk threads of reds, blues, greens, and yellows; the embroidery employs flat and satin stitches and also incorporates metallic gilt thread and small spangles.[27] In this example, Woodbury embraced familiar English iconography, with the overlay of Asian influence, such as vases of exotic flowers and flying phoenixes. Based on a record of the donation of this item, where it is described as "a baptismal apron embroidered in colors . . . done at a young ladies' finishing school in Boston," its creation is dated around 1735.[28]

Elizabeth Bull, another Boston woman of Mary Woodbury's generation, demonstrated her skill with embroidery on her wedding dress, which she began working on in 1731 or thereabouts, actually four years before her marriage.[29] No information survives about where she acquired her craft, whether from a female relative or one of those many female academies—or some combination of the two. The record does show that she had already lost her father—Jonathan Bull, whose property holdings included a tavern and a wharf—and that her inheritance made her a wealthy young woman. At her wedding, to Rev. Roger Price in 1735, the dress was still not quite complete: upon close inspection, one can see the hand-drawn patterns on the silk petticoat that had not yet been embroidered. For the embroidery, Elizabeth had used silk thread, applying it to the Chinese silk of the dress itself, once a celadon green and now much faded.

One determining factor in how a garment like this signaled the wearer's status was the quality of such colors. Because of their value, good dyes and skilled dyers could attract customers in a busy town like Boston. Along with stressing his connection to London in his 1729 advertisement, dyer James Vincent also touted his stock of prized pigments and that his shop "dyes and scours all sorts of women's wearing apparel, tabbies, mohairs, rich damasks, fine brocade . . . new dips Scarlet Cloth and Camblets, dyes cherry and grain colours, and Blews and Greens in silks."[30] Young women like Elizabeth Bull, socially prominent and with financial resources, would have valued the fashionable colors that a Boston tradesmen like Vincent made available. But such women also had the option of importing their wedding ensembles from London, as Bull may have and Rebecca Tailer (b. ca. 1718), also of Boston, most likely did.

At her wedding in 1747, Tailer wore emerald-green silk damask, the same luxurious color saturating both dress and shoes (page 38). While the survival of the ensemble is rare, the color is not: it has held fast to many shoes and dresses now in museum collections and was, apparently, a fashion favorite of the mid-eighteenth century. Indeed, how well the items have held their color suggests greater expense; even with careful stewardship, textiles with lesser-quality dyes can fade over 250 years.

FIG 1.8: Elizabeth Bull dress, courtesy of Revolutionary Spaces. See also Fig. I.14.

FIG 1.9a: Rebecca Tailer Byles dress, back, with shawl. Originally this dress included the length of pleated fabric, extending from the back of the neckline to the floor, characteristic of a sack-back gown. The garment appears to have been refashioned twice, circa 1770 and in the late 19th century. The neckline and sleeves were also altered.

For the front, see Fig. 1.9b, in following page spread; for detail of fabric, Fig. F.1.

FIG 1.10a, b: Shoes.

Both pieces—dress and shoes—suggest their likely costliness in other ways as well: the weight of the dress and its large-scale pattern repeat in the silk damask bespeak high-end textile production, such as that provided by Spitalfields in London. The pattern could be attributed to Anna Maria Garthwaite, an English designer whose work was much prized.[31] The pattern on the shoes, floral and well aligned, also suggests the skill of their creation, as do other distinctive touches—the fine stitching and the white rand, using that layer of textile between the outer sole and the fabric to create a flash of color contrast. These details alone would point to a London craftsperson, but good fortune has also preserved a label on one of the shoes, identifying cordwainer Robert Dasson (or Basson) of London as their maker.[32]

The origin and quality of Tailer's wedding clothes convey a great deal about the status of her families: her father, William Tailer (1676–1732), descended from wealthy landowners and merchants on both sides and served as lieutenant governor (see discussion of his waistcoat, p. 52), and her husband, Rev. Mather Byles, was among Boston's intellectual elite and a highly respected minister (for his purchase of gloves, see p. 70).[33] For both Elizabeth Bull Price and Rebecca Tailer Byles, the connection between colonial Boston and England would remain an important one. Generally for women of their class, the transatlantic market provided access to high-quality and high-profile goods to grace special occasions. For some, it also supported the family coffers, as British American merchants engaged in this profitable trade. But for Price and Byles there were other dimensions as well—trajectories that also involved their garments.

Elizabeth and Roger Price, who was English-born, moved their family to England in 1754.

She never returned to America, but her wedding dress did, traveling back with Elizabeth's daughter at some point after the Revolution. It then remained in the family until the time of its donation in 1910 to what was then the Bostonian Society (known today as Revolutionary Spaces). Before the donation, the dress had been altered at least twice—in the eighteenth and nineteenth centuries—for wear by subsequent family members.[34]

The partial dispersal of the family of Rebecca Byles has a more dramatic historic context: an ardent loyalist, Mather Byles incurred much disfavor in Boston as the Revolution came near.[35] Rebecca did not bear much of the family's ill fortune, as she passed away in 1773, while revolutionary tension was simmering but not yet boiling.[36] Reverend Byles lived another fifteen years in a community that now reviled his political opinions, and after his death in 1788 his and Rebecca's daughters, Mary and Catherine, remained in Boston, unapologetic loyalists. Their older brother, born of Reverend Byles's first marriage, fled to Canada. Continuing in the family house on Tremont Street, Mary and Catherine defended their nostalgia for the colonial era, until their deaths in 1832 and 1837, respectively. Despite their determined stewardship of all they had inherited, however, their mother's elegant wedding shoes and dress ended up with a family member in Brussels, returning to Boston when the Massachusetts Historical Society acquired them.[37] That acquisition enriched the connections between the written archival record—a large collection of family papers held at the Society—and the textile record.

FIG 1.9b
Facing,
FIG 2.12
Oliver
waistco

THE EMBELLISHED GENTLEMAN

ONE EVENING in January 1766, John Adams dined at the home of Boston merchant Nicholas Boylston (1716–1771). Still almost a decade away from his political career, Adams was at this time a thirty-year-old lawyer who had not traveled outside of New England. He was, as his diary attests, awed by the cosmopolitan opulence of Boylston's residence, known locally as "the Mansion House," situated in the province's urban center:

> An elegant Dinner indeed! Went over the House to view the Furniture, which alone costs a thousand Pounds sterling. A Seat it is for a noble Man, a Prince. The Turkey Carpets, the painted Hangings, the Marble Tables, the rich Beds with crimson Damask Curtains and Counterpins, the beautiful Chimny Clock, the Spacious Garden, are the most magnificent of any Thing I have ever seen.[1]

Although both men were born and raised within fifteen miles of each other, Boylston in Boston and Adams in Braintree, Adams's response to the older man's house underscores their differences. Adams seems to personify the thrifty and provincial New Englander. Even in the years following his international diplomatic service, including his tenure as president, he and his family remained relatively modest in their self-presentation and dedicated to maintaining the working farm that was also their home. Boylston, Adams's senior by twenty years, exuded instead the flair of the wealthy merchant, showing off in his home and on his person his access to luxury goods from around the globe.[2]

This image of New England self-fashioning is famously captured in the portrait of Boylston painted by the rising young artist John Singleton Copley in 1769. Here Boylston appears enrobed in a voluminous Indian-style banyan, or dressing gown, woven of lustrous brown silk damask, and capped with an Arabian-style tam, or turban.[3] Boylston was not unique in appropriating "exotic" garb to present himself as a citizen of the world. So, also, did other members of the Boylston family, such as brother Thomas and sister Rebecca, and other eminent residents of the town. These portraits do not conform to our ideas of provincial Americans, as we imagine them in the paintings of John and Abigail Adams (fig. I.6), Joseph Warren, or Jeremy Belknap, a New Hampshire minister and the founder of the

2.1: *Nicholas Boylston*, by John Singleton ~~ley~~, ca. 1769. Museum of Fine Arts, Boston. ~~tograph~~ © 2021 Museum of Fine Arts, Boston.

Massachusetts Historical Society.[4] Despite those differences, all of the families represented in these images belonged to a highly visible public realm. They would be seen, and therefore household resources were invested in proper attire for the gentlemen of the house.

vary considerably across class, region, and era. Unlike Nicholas Boylston's merchant showiness, the persona of the New England gentleman embodied by the likes of Adams, Warren, and Belknap suggests a more direct lineage from their seventeenth-century forebears—the men

By the seventeenth and eighteenth centuries, a man's outfit was usually an ensemble of three primary pieces, resembling the conventional business suit we are familiar with today. Eighteenth-century breeches, which might typically be made of cotton, silk, or leather, are recognizable to us today as pants or trousers; the waistcoat became a vest; and a frock coat is still just that—a coat. By the middle of the eighteenth century, even men's footwear began to look largely as it does today, with low heels, leather or suede texture, and muted colors, though this was a new trend: in England and Europe in the preceding centuries, elite men's shoes often sported brightly colored silk ribbons, metallic lace, and high heels.

Clothing for men, as for women, communicated a great deal about station, resources, and status. Of course, what was appropriate could

who had helped establish settlements in New England, many motivated by religious principles that separated them from the conventions of the English and Continental aristocracy.

Such a man was John Leverett (1616–1679), governor of the Massachusetts Bay Colony from 1673 to 1679, though his biography in some ways straddles the spectrum characterized by Adams and Boylston. Leverett was a religious nonconformist, a Puritan, who as a teenager immigrated to the colony with his family in 1633. Later ventures took him abroad again, some for business but most for diplomatic and military purposes, including several transatlantic trips during times of war and for significant appointments in England. The high esteem in which Leverett's peers held him was voiced by Cotton Mather, who described Leverett as "one to whom the Affections of the Freemen were signalized, in his quick advances through the lesser Stages of Office and Honour, unto the highest in the Country; and one whose Courage had been as much Recommended by Martial Actions abroad in his Younger Years, as his Wisdom and Justice were now at Home in his Elder."[5]

One article of Leverett's clothing, among the earliest and most historically significant items in the MHS textile collection, represents the martial aspect of Leverett's life: a buff coat, the name reflecting the use of leather from a buffalo or ox.[6] Although the maker is unknown, the garment probably dates from the 1640s at the latest, when Leverett was back in England fighting in the English civil war on the side of Oliver Cromwell and his Roundhead forces. In England, Leverett held a command in the regiment of Thomas Rainsborough, serving alongside other men from Massachusetts.[7] Leverett

also served in later expeditions on the eastern seaboard of North America, including enforcing English rule on French Acadian populations in Nova Scotia.[8]

A necessary garment for battle, Leverett's buff displays signs of hard use and distress from armed conflict, including scrapes, blood, and damage resulting from being pierced with a sharp weapon. A painting of Leverett, attributed to Sir Peter Lely, depicts him in this coat with his sword and family crest in the background. The painting confirms that the buff was once adorned with silver fastenings and also shows the kind of belt that Leverett wore with it. Constructed of several high-waisted panels, also called skirts, the coat still has a single belt loop, with evidence of another still visible. Cut-outs at the elbows and the cuffs feature ornamental scalloping and would have shown off a valuable

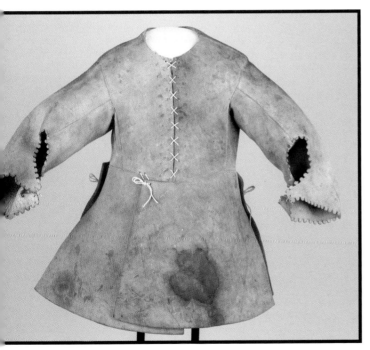

cing page, FIG 2.2: *John Adams*, by Benjamin Blyth. FIG 2.3: *Jeremy Iknap*, by Henry Sargent. FIG 2.4: *Joseph Warren*, by Edward Savage. ove, FIG 2.5a: John Leverett buff coat. Right, FIG 2.6: *John Leverett*, Sir Peter Lily (British). Peabody Essex Museum.,106819. © Peabody ex Museum, Salem, MA. Photograph by Mark Sexton.

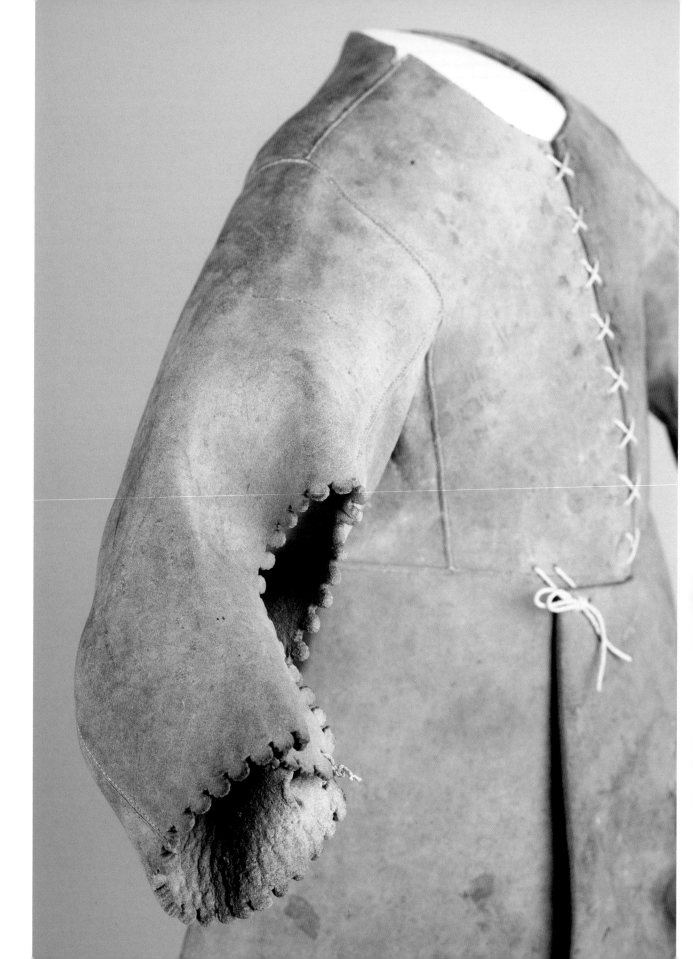

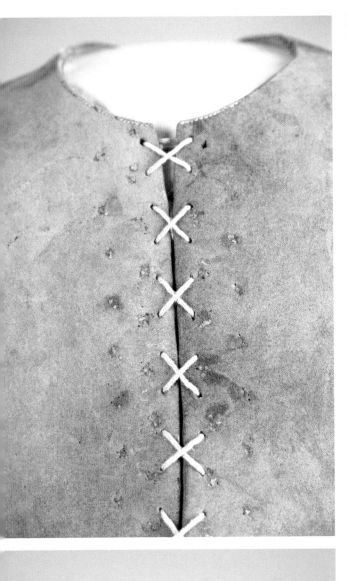

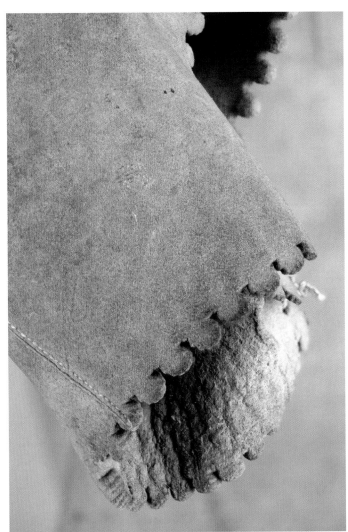

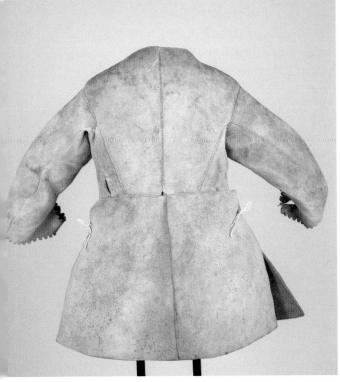

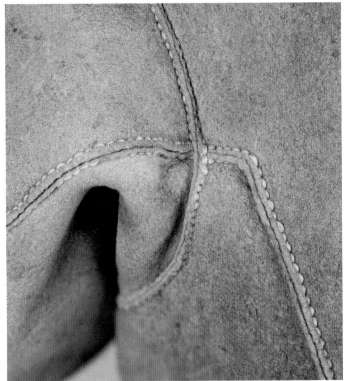

silk or fine linen shirt worn underneath. As typical decorative touches in the period, the cutouts added expense at the time, and today they demonstrate that ornament was not at odds with military purpose.

Adding a coat like this to one's battle kit was expensive, as we see in a letter from John Turberville to his father-in-law in 1640: "For your buff-coat I have looked after, and the price: they are exceedingly dear, not a good one to be gotten under £10, a very poor one for five or six pounds." At the same time, outfitting parliamentarian soldiers in standard buffs cost less than two pounds per.[9] Leverett may have acquired his garment while overseas, where he had opportunities to purchase textiles of the best quality and latest style (see pages 26 and 28 for Hannah Leverett's petticoat). Or he could have purchased it in Boston, where he also would have had access to imported goods from global markets.

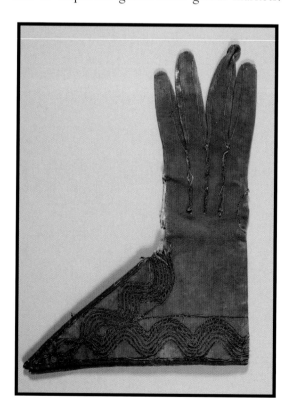

Indeed, by the 1660s, Massachusetts legislation stipulated buff coats as one option among the "corset" required for certain military service.[10] Of course, those worn by the typical pikeman may have been less ornate than Leverett's. Successful in his commercial venturea and a leader in Boston's governing elite, Leverett partook of the best quality available to the Boston elite.

Another gentleman's item that similarly combined function with embellishment belonged to William Stoughton, the acting royal governor of Massachusetts from 1694 to 1701. With a career that encompassed pastoral duties and provincial politics, Stoughton has the now dubious distinction of having served as chief justice of the witchcraft trials that took place in Massachusetts in 1692. A glove designed specifically to protect the hand and wrist in battle, also known as a *gauntlet*, this piece is hand sewn of red suede with a parchment-lined cuff that is also embroidered in gold metallic thread. The suede and the thread, which now appear dull, would have been vibrant when the gloves were new.

While we may think of women's clothing and accessories as more dramatic, more decorative than men's, in the seventeenth and eighteenth centuries male attire was frequently bolder and more luxurious. As the eighteenth century unfolded in colonial America, and restrictive Puritan conventions receded, even a New England man might wear garments featuring silk brocades and damasks, gold and silver braid, and surfaces

Preceding spread:
FIGS 2.5b: Leverett coat, right side; 2.5c-f: same, clockwise from upper right: front detail; right arm, detail; back left shoulder detail; back.

Left, FIG 2.7: William Stoughton glove.

Facing page, FIG 2.8a: Boylston family pocketbook, front, closed.

embroidered with metallic and silk threads and spangles. His accessories might be made of the softest Moroccan leathers and goatskins. These luxuries were of course beyond the reach of Everyman, but for the elite, garments constructed at a certain level of quality were expected as a demonstration of their social position.

Consider, again, the trappings chosen by Nicholas Boylston for his life in Boston, some three thousand miles from what he may have thought to be the centers of "civilization"—London, Paris, and Amsterdam.[11] Beginning the day at his sumptuous home on School Street, Boylston would awaken in a room that was filled with objects imported from across the globe—perhaps in an English-made bed crafted of rosewood from China or mahogany from Brazil, ornamented with those "crimson Damask Curtains" that John Adams admired.[12] Possibly he

would have donned the brown banyan depicted in Copley's painting, a type of item that was often woven in India of fine silk from China. As he made his daily rounds in town, he perhaps carried the extant, lushly embellished wallet attributed to the Boylston family, although not to any one family member. An accessory appropriate for an elite merchant like Nicholas, it features metallic thread embroidery and interior leather finish work of the highest quality.

Another wallet, embroidered with the name "Benjamin Stuart" and the date 1753, gives a sense of what a man of more modest means would have carried. Vibrant and fanciful, this wallet is not professionally crafted but homemade and richly embroidered with crewel (wool thread) on linen. The brightly hued pastoral view includes vining flowers, a bird, and goats; several large blossoms catch the eye. Both the outside

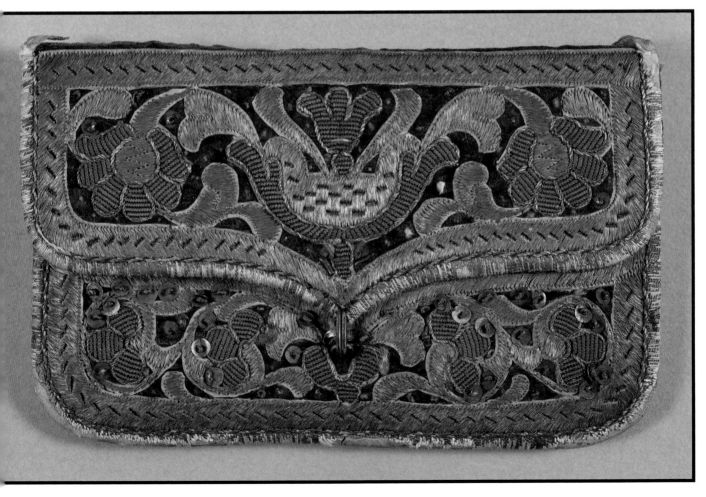

Left and above, FIG 2.8b, c: Boylston pocketbook, front open; back.

Left, below, FIG 2.9a: Stuart pocketbook, back.

Facing page, FIG 2.9b: Stuart pocketbook, front. For the interior of this item, see Figs. I.7 and B.2.

threads and the interior lining of yellow-gold silk, possibly from China, have remained vivid. The large size of the pocketbook was fashioned to accommodate old tenor currency. Although no information exists to help identify the maker, the owner may have been Capt. Benjamin Stewart (ca. 1730–1775), who spent most of his adult life in military service and was on the verge of fighting in the Revolutionary War when he died of smallpox in 1775.[13] It may have been made for him by Deborah Ryder, who married Benjamin in 1754. Young women often made items like this, sometimes for themselves but just as often for their fathers or beloveds.

The colorful and vibrant textiles and needlework on display in these accessories also had their place on the eighteenth-century gentleman's waistcoat, a primary garment for demonstrating a man's position in society. Indeed, its immediate predecessor, the "vest," became required court attire in 1666 by order of King

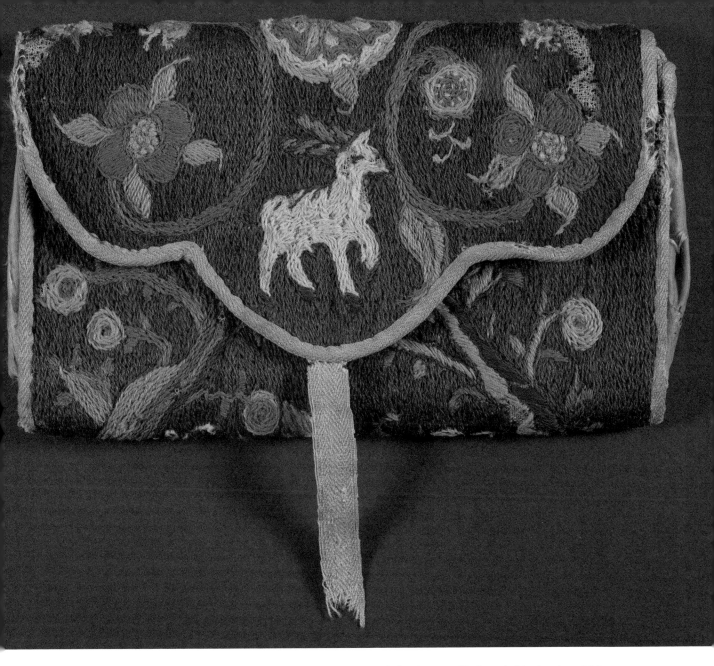

Charles II, as Samuel Pepys noted in his diary on October 8 of that year.[14] A week later, Pepys recorded the first appearance of the king and his courtiers in the new suit:

> This day the King begins to put on his vest, and I did see several persons of the House of Lords and Commons too, great courtiers, who are in it; being a long cassocke close to the body, of black cloth, and pinked with white silke under it, and a coat over it, and the legs ruffled with black riband like a pigeon's leg; and, upon the whole, I wish the King may keep it, for it is a very fine and handsome garment.[15]

Eventually the "long cassocke" shortened to waist length, sometimes with sleeves, sometimes without.

By the eighteenth century, as waistcoats became de rigueur for gentlemen in England and colonial North America, its broad adoption allowed for standardized construction. Waistcoat panels were purchased and then sewn together to make a good fit for the new owner. But this standardization did not inhibit its use as a prime garment for individual expression—and especially displays of wealth, good taste, and access to global markets.

In early eighteenth-century Boston, gentlemen like William Tailer (1676–1731) epitomized that intersection. Descending on both sides from early New England families—Tailer and Stoughton—William inherited wealth and social prominence. His own endeavors cemented his social position through civil and military service, culminating in several terms as lieutenant governor and acting governor after 1711.[16] His stunning embroidered waistcoat, likely made sometime between 1720 and 1730, is replete with metallic thread and spangles. This is a complex piece, signifying the refinements that his station called for. The embroidery, laid on a heavy white or off-white silk, is set off against naturalistic rococo floral motifs, featuring some especially subtle shading of the leaves and flowers. The waistcoat includes actual pockets, rather than the typical ornamental pocket flaps. Gold foil backs the coat's buttons, their wood core festooned in metallic thread. The buttonholes are meticulously finished, also with gold thread. The waistcoat is in fine condition and most likely from England or from France, where nameless embroiderers toiled for scant pay received by the piece, which was the usual practice. Inspection reveals the garment was later altered—let out at the sides and along the neck and shoulders to accommodate Tailer's growing bulk or perhaps to fit a new owner. Although the alterations were skillfully done, the public would not view them, as a gentleman like Tailer ordinarily would not have removed his jacket before the "middling sort" or, indeed, any person other than his intimates.

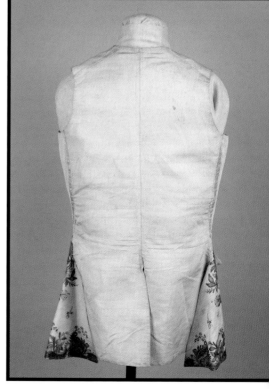

FIG 2.10, a-c: William Tailer waistcoat.
See also Figs. 1.9a and b for detail.

FIG 2.11: *Andrew Oliver, Jr.*, by Joseph Blackburn. Reproduction Courtesy of the Oliver Family.

FIG 2.12b, c: Andrew Oliver, Jr., waistcoat. See also page 41.

Facing page, FIG 2.13: Henry Bromfield wig set, clockwise from top: the wig; a leather pouch for dusting powder; a powder puff, made of a coiled upholstery fringe sewn together at the woven base; a black silk queue bag; and a coconut shell container.

Born the year that Tailer died, Andrew Oliver, Jr. (1731–1799), exemplified the well-dressed gentleman of his generation, as evidenced by a sleeved waistcoat that survives from his wardrobe and that is featured in his portrait as painted by Joseph Blackburn in 1755 (although Blackburn exercised artistic license in his depiction of the waistcoat). Exquisitely fashioned of blue silk embroidered with silver gilt decoration, this garment was most likely made in England. The silk is "figured," the pattern emerging from the "tone on tone" weaving of the blue thread.

At the time that the painting was made, Oliver was still a young man, only twenty-four or twenty-five, and had married Mary Lynde in 1752—the same year he earned a master's degree from Harvard. Despite his youth, he was already a gentleman of means, having inherited substantial properties even before beginning college. His professional life before an appointment to the Court of Common Pleas in 1761 consisted of various municipal offices, including those of constable and selectman.[17] As Oliver's girth increased over the years, his blue waistcoat grew as well: a tailor supplemented the original cut with extra pieces of fabric to expand it, evidenced by additions to the back and the sleeves. Much later (and hastily), someone altered the sleeves—likely the result of descendants using the garment for fancy dress or a Colonial Revival pageant.

Aside from a central garment such as the waistcoat, a gentleman also relied upon an armory of accessories and articles of personal adornment—the small things that provided the finishing touch, the polish to an ensemble: change purses and pocketbooks, such as the Boylston family's; buckles for shoes and breeches; snuff boxes and jewelry; various military regalia and equine equipage; perfumes, such as lavender water, and lozenges to hide odors and sweeten the breath; and, of course, the once ubiquitous formal powdered wig, or peruke, which may strike us as comical today but was essential in the eighteenth century. Because some of these small vanities suggested excess, they could arouse popular criticism. Gentlemen's luxuries were not as routinely condemned in the press, depicted as seeking to deceive or being overly lavish, as were women's, but men who seemed too extravagant were nonetheless considered foppish or effeminate and came in for their own share of ridicule. A prime target of such lampooning was the gentleman's wig and especially the accoutrements for its care—the powder, bought by the pound; the pomade for cleaning and styling; and the time spent with a manservant preparing the wig for public viewing.

Most of what we know about wigs today is from printed and painted depictions. Such headdresses rarely survived the passage of time, leaving us with few extant examples of these once common items to examine. Fortunately, an ex-

cmplary peruke was donated to the MHS along with an unusually complete set of masculine attire that belonged to Boston merchant Henry Bromfield (1727–1820), addressed fondly in the latter part of his life as "the Colonel" in recognition of his militia service during the Revolutionary War. Bromfield's ensemble includes not only his European-made wig but also its related accessories: coconut-shell container, leather powder bag with dusting puff, and pouch for the wig's long braid, known as the *queue*. The quality of Bromfield's black silk pouch, used to keep a gentleman's coat and collar clean, establishes the formality of Bromfield's wig accoutrement.

In its construction, Bromfield's peruke exemplifies the type appropriate for his station. Most wigs were white or gray, and his is gray, the color typical for a man in business.[18] Also like most eighteenth-century wigs, it comprises three distinct areas of construction—top, sides, and queue—variously made up of horse hair and human hair, used separately (horse hair alone for the queue) or in combination (for the rest). While horse hair imported from China went into most wigs, those of the best quality used human hair specifically from Northern European peasant girls, as the climate and diet were believed to provide a better product than the less expensive alternatives: hair from criminals, plague victims, or even cadavers. Aside from the hair itself, woven and sewn in layers, a complex construction of other materials created and maintained the necessary shape: linen for the hand-knotted base layer, referred to as the *caul* or *netting*; linen again for a lining between the netting and the wearer's head; metal (lead in this case) for small stays between those two layers; and pink silk for a tape that ran along the interior edge.

In addition to Bromfield's wig, the wardrobe donated to the MHS comprises his tricorn hat, knee breeches, shoe buckles, cane, and red cloak, which makes his the most complete set of eighteenth- to early nineteenth-century clothing in the Society's holdings. Even during his own lifetime, Colonel Bromfield was recognized for his standard outfit, which he still wore regularly in his last years, an icon of a bygone era. Indeed, Bromfield's presentation was so remarkable, and so beloved by those close to him, that descriptions have been passed down in manuscripts and books, noting the items preserved today.

In her journal for 1816, Eliza Susan Quincy recorded a visit that she and her mother made to Bromfield at his country home in Harvard, Massachusetts. "We paused at the gate to look back at the house," Eliza wrote, "when its door opened & uncle Bromfield in his red cloak & cocked hat, on the top of a wig, came out and advanced toward us. —It was a complete picture of past times." His grandson Henry Bromfield Rogers carried a similar picture in his memory: "I see him now in his large powdered wig, his square brown coat and vest, with broad pockets and lappets, black small-clothes, nice silk stockings, silver knee-buckles, and gold-headed cane."[19]

Aside from being a patriot and a beloved figure in his community, Bromfield was also a trader in textiles—specifically English cloth, as well as ribbons and sundries. Chief among the items he left to posterity is that red cloak, made of a superfine wool imported from England and possibly made up domestically, perhaps between 1790 and 1810.[20] It has a collar band with red satin ribbon to tie it closed, and it shows evidence of alteration at the front, under the collar, perhaps to shorten it for a later owner. It is an almost perfect example of a once ubiquitous outer garment that reflects everyday life in early Massachusetts.

These eye-catching protective covers held a place of pride and practicality for both men and women, of rich means and modest, in the fashions of early America. They were common items that would be seen in cloakrooms and on hooks lining a wall. A wintry New England day called for a heavy wool garment. Of course, not all of the cloaks worn in seventeenth- and eighteenth-century New England were scarlet—many if not most would have been brown, black, or gray. But the red added a spot of brightness to bleak days, and it appears that these examples engaged the interest of later generations, as a preponderance of red cloaks has survived. Today, we find similar items in museum collections and also represented in written records such as probate inventories. Other red cloaks that survived the ravages of time are housed at the Metropolitan Museum of Art, the Los Angeles County Museum of Art, the Saco Museum, Historic Deerfield, and Colonial Williamsburg.

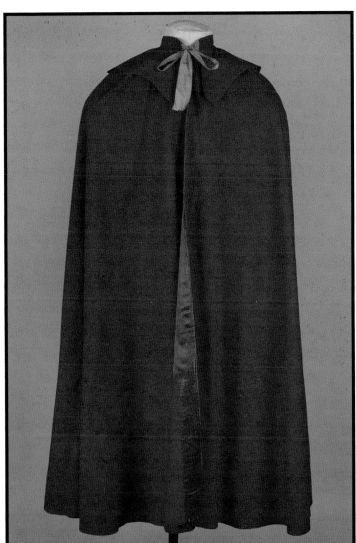

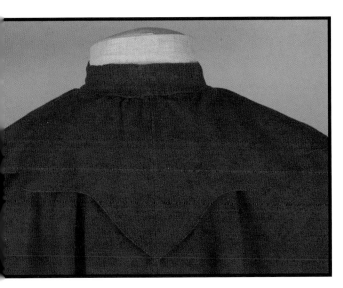

FIG 2.14a-c: Henry Bromfield wool cloak.

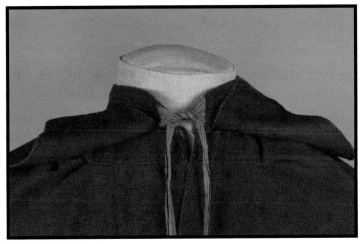

Another example also resides at the MHS, a slightly earlier piece, made around 1770, that belonged to Peter Oliver (1713–1791), who was chief justice of the Superior Court in Massachusetts and a member of both the House of Representatives and the Governor's Council, as well as uncle to Andrew Oliver, Jr.[21] Oliver's cape shows a level of quality appropriate for a man of such stature: composed of a fine textile, bright in color and well tailored, it features a high degree of top-notch finish work. Oliver's cloak predates Bromfield's by at least twenty years and, most significantly, was a Revolutionary-era creation. Befitting an eminent, fashion-conscious Tory at

that time, Oliver likely imported his garment from England, perhaps through the Long Wharf trading house held in concert with his brother Andrew Oliver, Sr. (1706–1774). The cloak is fitted with a two-stage double collar: the top can fold upright and button at the neck, while the lower collar is scalloped, ending in a point at center back. Against the bitter winds of Revolutionary Boston, Peter Oliver could draw up the collar about his neck for warmth.

As political tensions rose in Massachusetts in the 1760s, Oliver found himself more and more at odds with his peers and with the common sentiment. Like his brother, Peter was an ardent loyalist, but Andrew died in 1774, thus spared the ensuing years of conflict. Peter went to the heart of it, refusing to forgo his duties as justice, even under the threat of mob violence, and serving in the Mandamas Council, a body appointed by royal writ in lieu of the elected representatives of the provincial legislature. Becoming a target of the patriots, Peter Oliver found by 1776 that he was no longer safe in Massachusetts and so left, first, for Nova Scotia and then for England.

FIG 2.15a-d: Peter Oliver wool cloak.

SEVERAL DECADES earlier, and about five hundred miles south of Boston, a teenaged George Washington had begun copying adages from gentility manuals into his now-famous notebook, "Rules of Civility and Decent Behavior: In Company and Conversation." For Rule Number 54, the future first president wrote, "Play not the peacock, looking every where about you, to see if you be well decked, if your shoes fit well, if your stockings sit neatly and clothes handsomely."[22] By including this among the guidelines he continued to consult as he matured, Washington demonstrated his appreciation for the significance of clothing for gentlemen in the eighteenth century.

When George married Martha (Dandridge) Custis in January 1759, he became stepfather to Martha's four-year-old son, John Parke Custis.[23] As such, he became responsible for many aspects of the boy's care, including guiding him in matters of clothing and decorum. This would be particularly true once Jacky, as he was known in the family, was "breeched"—a boy's transition, usually between the ages of four and eight, from wearing a kind of skirt common to boys and girls to his first pants, known as *breeches*. According to prevailing tradition, Jacky would now spend more time in his stepfather's sphere than he had in early childhood, when he inhabited the domestic circle of his mother.[24]

This shift hewed to a gendered division of responsibility for household expenses, particularly for textiles, that prevailed in American homes as it did in English. Where the female head of household saw to clothing the women and girls as well as the young boys, the male head of household took over for boys as they grew, as well as for male servants.[25] The level of care that Washington maintained in these responsibilities comes through in a 1764 order to Charles Law-

rence, in which Washington specified, in exquisite detail, a "Livery suit" of

> worsted Shagg of the Inclosed colour & fineness lined with red Shalloon—and made as follows—The Coat and Breeches alike with a plain white washed button—the Button holes worked with Mohair of the same colr—A Collar of red shagg to the Coat with a narrow lace like the Inclosed round it—a narrow Cuff of the same colour of the Coat turn'd up to the bent of the Arm and laced round at that part—the waistcoat made of red Shagg (worsted shagg also) and laced with the same lace as that upon the Collar and Sleeves.[26]

Many such orders for garments show up frequently in his correspondence, demonstrating both his keen knowledge of textile matters and his expectations as to the quality of the finished work.[27]

For Washington, his larger role as stepfather meant teaching his charge how a young gentleman should appear in the broader world. Accordingly, he ordered clothing for Jacky appropriate to the boy's age in any given year and also consistent with the style and level of quality he would order for himself. In 1768, Washington placed one of his orders with Lawrence describing items both for his own wardrobe and for his stepson's. He began with his own outfit:

> This is to desire you will send me a Suit of handsome Cloth Cloaths—I have no doubts but you will choose a fashionable colourd Cloth as well as a good one & make it in the best taste to sit easy & loose as Cloaths that are tight always look aukward & are uneasy to the Wearer.

The ensuing paragraph sets out items appropriate for a thirteen-year-old youth and his manservant:

You are also desired to send the following Cloaths for Mastr Custis—to wit—a handsome Suit of fashionable Cloth—Also a riding dress of green Cloth. . . . likewise send for his Man a Suit of blew Livery—the Servt is abt five feet 8 Inches high & Slender.[28]

Similarly, when Jacky was a young man of seventeen Washington sent a list of items to Thomas Gibson that included for himself "A Fashe Suit of Cloaths, made of a handsome, Superfe Broad Cloth for dress," and for Jacky "A Fashe Suit of Cloaths made of a handsome Super[fin]e brd Cloath for dress"; for himself "A Fashe Ditto [suit of clothes] made of Cassimer for Summer Wear—well fancied & only faced & Lined in the foreskirts," and for Jacky "A Fashe & handse Suit of D[itt]o for Summer Wear to be faced & Lined in the Foreskirts only." For each he also ordered "A Riding Frock," his to be paired with "A Riding Waistcoat of Superfine Scarlet Cloth—and gold Lace" and Jacky's with a "Buffcloath Waistt wt. a gold Lace." Among a few other last items, he also ordered for each of them a pair of "Silk Nett Breeches."[29]

On the same day—July 15, 1772—that Washington sent the above specifications to Gibson, he also sent an order for shoes to John Didsbury. Here his descriptions point out the differences between what he wanted for himself and what his charge—who undoubtedly had his own opinions preferred. "Mr. Custis," he wrote, "desires his Shoes may be made long & low in the hind Quarters—In short that they may be made fashionable." Conversely, he also observed that a pair previously made for his own use were "very ill shap'd; at least they do not please my taste as I am not fond of either long, or low hind Quarters, or sharp Toes." Communicating his stepson's order so clearly, and distinctly at odds

with his own less fashionable choices, Washington recognizes seventeen-year-old Jacky's transition into adulthood.[30]

Possibly the most important statement that Washington would make in his choice of clothing came after the war, when he became the first president of the new nation. For his 1789 inauguration ceremony in New York, he chose an unostentatious suit, one of broadcloth most likely made by a manufacturer recently established in Connecticut.[31] He also favored similar styles during his tour of the United States later that year, demonstrating the importance of wearing—and purchasing—American-made textiles. With these suits, he appeared to reflect on a debate that emerged during the Revolution and had a powerful effect on American self-fashioning and industry. Should patriots demonstrate their independence from British culture, and goods, by favoring domestic manufactures, such as "homespun" textiles? Or did the new nation need to demonstrate its legitimacy in the international realm by maintaining its cultural connection with the British Empire?

Following page spread:

FIG 2.16: Frederic Baury vest, ca. 1809-1812.

FIG 2.17: Folding chair made using the red cloak John Adams wore while in England, 1784-1785.

FIG 3.1: *George Washington*, attributed to Jane Stuart.

FASHIONING REVOLUTIONARY SENTIMENT

GEORGE WASHINGTON understood the significance of public self-presentation. With the many orders for suits and shoes he placed for himself and his household, he was exacting about the details—cloth, linings, lace, buttonholes—and attentive to propriety and social position. So in the months leading up to his (expected) inauguration as the nation's first president in 1789, his deliberate effort to secure American-made cloth for a new suit suggests the meaning he believed the brown broadcloth would convey on April 30.[1]

Three months earlier, he addressed a letter to his fellow soldier and trusted advisor Henry Knox with some new orders:

> Having learnt from an Advertisement in the New York Daily Advertiser, that there were superfine American Broad Cloths to be sold at No. 44 in Water Street; I have ventured to trouble you with the Commission of purchasing enough to make me a suit of Cloaths.

Washington continued with more details, regarding dye and twist for button holes, and then noted that if the material could not be found at the shop in New York, "quere could they be had from Hartford in Connecticut where I perceive a Manufactury of them is established."[2] This new establishment, a harbinger of the industry the new nation might achieve and a key to its independence, became a thread in Washington's correspondence in the ensuing months.

Knox, in fact, found the New York shop empty of the desired cloth. "I immediately sent to the store where the american cloths were advertised for sale," he wrote on February 12, "and to all other stores where it was probable there were any, but was exceedingly chagrined to learn there were none in Town at present." He followed up four days later to report that "The cloths have not yet arrived although expected by the first wind," then noting in the next paragraph that "It appears by the returns of elections hitherto obtained . . . that your Excellency has every vote for President." By February 19, Knox had a partial victory, procuring and sending on "13 ½ yards of ¾ Wide bottle green cloth of the Hartford manufacture—I would there were more of it for your and Mrs Washingtons purposes but it was all of the color which came." In his letter of March 5, Knox conveyed news of "the assembling of the government the members of it who are in Town met together," closing the short note with the further comment that "Colonel Wadsworth informs me that he shall have here next week some superfine brown Hartford cloth intended for you."[3]

Colonel Wadsworth was Jeremiah Wadsworth, a former delegate to the Continental Congress and now a congressman from Connecticut in the House of Representatives; he was also, with Peter Colt, a founder of the Hartford Woolen Manufactory (HWM). Ultimately, Washington's effort to clothe himself in American self-sufficiency intersected with Wadsworth and Colt's desire to make the business a patriotic concern. By late March, the HWM proprietors had determined to give Hartford-made suits to both Washington and his impending vice president, John Adams.[4] In an April 8 letter to Daniel Hinsdale, the HWM agent who sent him the cloth, Washington acknowledged the gift—"make my warmest acknowledgments acceptable to the Directors for this mark of their politness and attention"—and continued,

> I am extremely pleased to find that the useful manufactures are so much attended to in our Country, and with such a prospect of success. . . . I am fully persuaded that if the spirit of industry economy and patriotism, which seems now beginning to dawn, should exert itself to a proper latitude, that we shall very soon be able to furnish ourselves at least with every necessary and useful fabrick. . . . —I shall allways take a peculiar pleasure in giving every proper encouragement in my power to the manufactures of my Country.[5]

Washington's attention to the political meaning of his attire for the new nation reflected a decades long tension over manufacturing and independence.

Although that tension had been detectable at least as early as the 1760s, before then domestic production of textiles would not have carried quite the same meaning for colonials in British America.[6] Mostly comfortable, or even eager, to demonstrate their connection to England, they prized their access to goods made in England and shipped to America—or even goods made elsewhere but traded by English merchants. While the sense of being British American could cut across classes, the colonies' most powerful families were especially covetous of the validation of their rightful place in the wider circle of British elite.

Consequently, even by the mid-eighteenth century, most British Americans saw no harm in indulging themselves with imported luxuries they could afford. In fact, it would prove to be a habit that was difficult to give up even when political conflict began to emerge and with it a strong and deliberate effort to encourage colonials away from depending on English goods.[7] With the new import tariffs implemented by the Sugar Act, the Stamp Act, and the Townshend Acts, colonists saw an opportunity to use boycotts as a form of protest, seeking to redirect their purchasing power to domestic producers and away from English purses—and especially the king's.

Over this same stretch of the 1760s, judgments about the nature of luxury as associated with foreign imports and home production (be it in the home or, simply, on domestic soil) circulated in the press. Some papers reprinted—at times slightly altered—choice quotations drawn from *The Querist*, an extensive list of questions published in the 1730s by George Berkeley that reflected on British politics in Ireland. In 1764, for example, the *Newport Mercury* published four

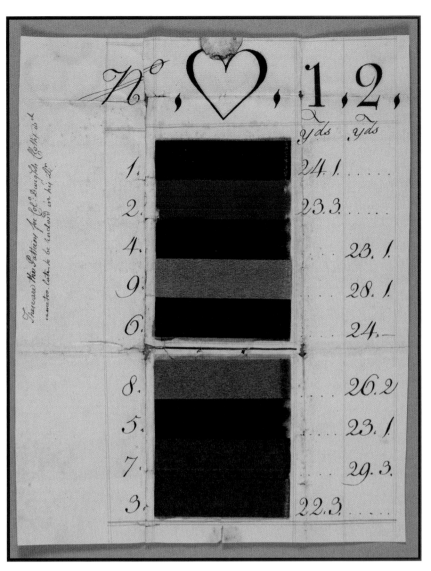

Based on the handwriting and the three individuals named on this document, this set of swatches appears to be from the first half of the 18th century, possibly circa 1745.

Research suggests that two of the people mentioned, Henry Leddel and "Capt. Hollowell," were loyalists who later left Boston during the evacuation by the British in 1776.

In 1745, Leddel was beginning his career as merchant in Boston. Benjamin Hallowell was a prominent citizen who had earned a reputation for besting French privateers and who currently served as Comptroller of the Boston Custom House. The Col. Dwight for whom the samples were intended may have been Joseph Dwight (1703-1765), a colonel in a provincial militia until he became a brigadier general in 1745. There are, however, many Col. Dwights to be found in the family's genealogy.

For Leddel, see *The Robert Treat Paine Papers*, 1:195n1. For Hallowell, see Sandra Webber, "Benjamin Hallowell Family and the Jamaica Plain House," website of the Jamaica Plain Historical Society. For Dwight, see *The History of the Descendants of John Dwight, of Dedham, Mass.*, by Benjamin Woodbridge Dwight (New York: John F. Trow & Son, 1874), 2:625.

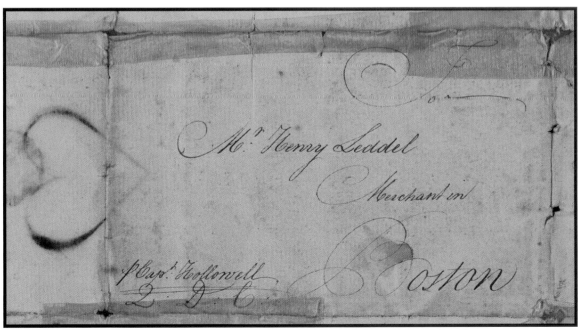

FIG 3.2a: Fabric samples, interior, as sent to Henry Leddel, merchant.

FIG 3.2b: Exterior of the sample packet with delivery instructions.

queries that directly equated imported luxury textiles with damage to the local well-being:

> Whether we are not undone by fashions made for other people and whether it be not madness in a poor people to imitate a rich one?
>
> Whether a woman of fashion not be declared a public enemy?
>
> Whether a lady set out with foreign silks and laces may not be said to consume more beef and butter than a hundred farmers?[8]

A few weeks later, the *New Hampshire Gazette* reproduced on its front page a Berkeley query that urged the value of in-home textile production, even if those products were for "embellishment" rather than just frugally utilitarian:

> Whether the women may not sew, spin, weave, Embroider, sufficiently for the embellishment of their persons, and even enough to raise Envy in each other, without being beholden to foreign countries?[9]

In this same year, an initiative to encourage production in the colonies was founded by a group of prominent New Yorkers who put it forward as the Society for the Promotion of Arts, Agriculture, and Economy. In statements printed in newspapers throughout the colonies, the group bemoaned "the present state of declining trade" and "the vast luxury introduced during the late [*Seven Years'*] war." Appealing to "every real Friend and Lover of his Country, . . . of whatever Rank or Condition," the communication criticized the Sugar Act—imposed on the colonial economy the preceding spring—and urged positive action to improve local industry. At the end of the year, voices in Rhode Island and New York papers hoped that pursuit of "some happy expedients will be discovered to check the progress of our luxury and extravagance."[10]

A serious and organized approach to the mechanized production of textiles was apparent in the colonies in the ensuing years. The next decade shows evidence of cotton card, linen, and wool manufactures established and/or producing textiles. In 1765, ten years before the Revolutionary War began, the *Boston Gazette* announced that,

> At the linnen manufactory in Boston, there has been made within these three last months 400 yards of Bengals, Lilleputias and Broglios, which have been bought by some of the principal Ladies in this Town, for their own and their Childrens wear And

FIG 3.3: Dress fashions for 1775, from the memorandum book of Elizabeth Price, daughter of Elizabeth Bull Price.

as the Ladies have set the Example I hope the Gentlemen will follow, as they may be supply'd in the Spring with several Sorts of Summer Wear by John Browne.[11]

A few years later, a set of patriotic Bostonians invested in a Roxbury clothier that was poised to begin production of wool broadcloth suits for men. The November 1767 notice reads, "We are assured that a Number of Gentlemen have advanced considerable to a Clothier in Roxbury, who has engaged to deliver in three Months ten suits of as fine Homespun Broad Cloth, as can be bought of British for £.10 per Yard."[12] That this was a patriotic gesture, and not simply a matter of frugality, is revealed in the remainder of the notice:

> We now learned that the Southern Colonies, as well as the People of New-England, much approve of the late Measures taken by this Metropolis. Town-Meetings are called and calling to promote Frugality and Manufactures, as the best Method to convince our Master Country of their Mistakes; or to save ourselves from the Destruction that threatens us, by saving our Money. . . .
>
> Those Towns who are most in earnest to banish Extravagance, and encourage Manufactures, must certainly soon be in the best Circumstances; and those Provinces which most heartily come into the present Measures, must undoubtedly before long be justly esteemed the most flourishing and happy.

Throughout the decade, as Britain's rule further curtailed colonists' self-government, Americans had to choose how to conduct their business—and consider the source of their garments and the materials involved in their construction.

On the side of those who wished to assert the rights of British Americans to dispute legislation imposed by Parliament, efforts to undermine the tariffs and regulations became paramount. In the decade before the war, these took the form of embargoes against British imports, particularly a series of non-importation agreements forged among merchants and retailers who promised not to sell the despised goods. The first of these, adopted in response to the Stamp Act in 1765, achieved its objective in less than a year when Parliament repealed the legislation. In the ensuing years, similar efforts pushed back against the Townshend Acts, and by 1770, Parliament's response left only one of these tariffs in place—the tariff levied on tea.

Early that same year, Bostonians Isaac and Mary Vibird found themselves at odds with the patriot sentiment regarding imported tea, and they used domestically produced footwear as an escape from criticism. Mary had come under attack for, allegedly, buying tea from an importer; Isaac sought to remove the suspicion with a public letter swearing that she was in the shop for "a Number of Shoes from Lynn."[13] Maintaining an image as a patriot sympathizer by disassociating from British goods and promoting domestic industry clearly required a great deal of care and was crucial in the charged political atmosphere. These bits of evidence also point toward the importance—political and economic—of the growing footwear manufactory in Massachusetts.

"Women's callimanco Shoes Lynn-made, as neat, and much stronger than any imported from England," read an advertisement in the *Boston Evening Post* in 1765.[14] The message to Boston customers is clear—shoes made in America are as good as and sturdier than those from England. The quantity of production at Lynn was also notable, with an output of eighty thousand pairs in 1767. The popularity of Lynn-made shoes even spread to London.[15]

As satisfying as this example of local production must have been to Massachusetts patriots, the reality of the manufacture—especially for calamanco shoes—undermines the idealized picture of the self-sufficient colonial household. Indeed, the very notion of an "age of homespun" coalesced in the Colonial Revival movement and was thus a creation of the end of the nineteenth century and the start of the twentieth.[16] There were, of course, limits to self-sufficiency in colonial New England and the early republic. Like so many products embedded in global trade routes, "Lynn-made" shoes were not wholly American made and largely relied on wool produced in Norwich, England—a process akin to the contemporary practice of assembling a car in the United States from individual components that originated in other countries.[17]

In the decade leading up to the Revolution, not all New Englanders were politically aligned with the patriot causes. In Boston, for example, the population of loyalists—colonials maintaining their allegiance to the Crown—included many prominent citizens. These families specifically transformed their fashion choices from mere displays of taste to political statements that matched in boldness those statements expressed by patriots. The Boylstons, Byleses, and Olivers, for example, continued to purchase luxury British goods despite—or to spite—non-importation agreements, newspaper editorials, and neighbors' laments. They adapted to the political challenges, purchasing from each other, as Mather Byles did when he bought his kidskin gloves from fellow loyalist Ralph Inman (see Figs. I.2a and b). He purchased English gloves even when they were specifically in violation of non-importation agreements. The general knowledge of Byles's lack of sympathy for independence led to severe consequences, including dismissal from his pulpit at the Hollis Street Church in 1776 and conviction the following year under a new law criminalizing criticism of the patriot cause. However, Byles managed to evade the deportation imposed upon many of his peers, enduring instead several years of house arrest.[18]

While loyalists like Byles continued to purchase British-made goods on principle, many New Englanders who supported the move toward domestic production also still purchased imports. Personal taste and the desire to look fashionable and genteel continued to be powerful motivators, and many of these luxuries had been so essential to British American identity for more than a hundred years that breaking with them proved to be easier said than done.

Abigail and John Adams were, of course, among the most ardent patriots in New England. Both devoted much of their lives to American independence. Among the personal sacrifices they made were the long stretches of separation, when John served in the Continental Congress in Philadelphia and, later, when he traveled to Europe as a minister of the new nation. For much of this time, Abigail remained on the family's property in Braintree, near Boston and therefore also close to the violence in the early years of the Revolutionary War.

The correspondence between John and Abigail is a key record of the history of the Revolution, and Abigail's reports from Braintree document many aspects of the "homefront" experience, including how the war disrupted access to goods. In July 1775, as British forces blocked shipping during the Siege of Boston, Abigail detailed the scarcity of many household staples: "You can hardly imagine how much we want many common small articles, which are not manufactured amongst ourselves." In the same July 16 letter, after stressing how difficult it was for Bostonians to procure food, she entreated John to try to send sundry items to her in Braintree, including calamanco: "Every article here in the West india way is very scarce and dear. In six weeks we shall not be able to purchase any article of the kind. I wish you would let Bass get me one pound of peper, and 2 yd. of black caliminco for Shooes."[19] Clearly, not all goods could be had locally, and even devoted patriots depended on global trade routes.

Abigail's observations on the shortage of goods at home, and the consequent high prices, reflect another aspect of her work during the Revolution. In her enterprising and matter-of-fact way, Abigail made use of her broadening network to bring scarce goods to the area during the Siege. From Philadelphia, where Congress was sitting, John was able to supply her with an order of a thousand pins, a request that she first described as "Something like the Barrel of Sand suppose you will think it, but really of much more im-

portance to me." Far from being sand, pins were in fact an indispensable item for clothing before the advent of hooks and snaps. She wanted, specifically, "a bundle of pins," explaining that "The cry for pins is so great that what we used to Buy for 7.6 are now 20 Shillings and not to be had for that."[20] A month later, in her July 16 letter, she reiterated the request: "Not one pin is to be purchased for love nor money. I wish you could convey me a thousand by any Friend travelling this way."[21]

As John's work took him farther away, Abigail's trading opportunities expanded. With his diplomatic appointments in Europe, John arranged shipments home comprising all manner of textiles, gloves, handkerchiefs, and ribbons, which she then sold through intermediaries. In a letter directed to John in Paris in 1780, Abigail mentioned that "you might if you pleased order remitted in common calico low priced hankerchiefs and fans which are articles that turn to the best account here" and declared that "The remit-

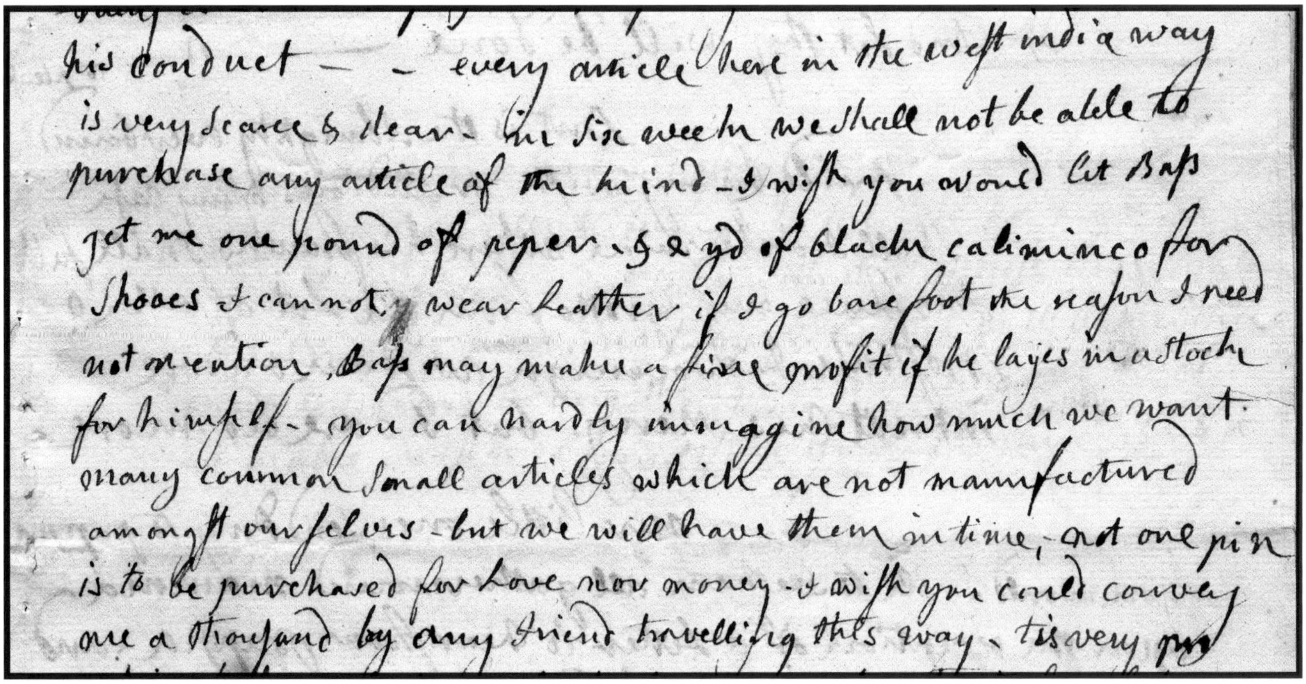

FIG 3.4: Abigail Adams to John Adams, July 16, 1775, p. 5.

tance from Bilboa will render me very comfortable for this 12 month."[22] In the same missive, she did request additional items for herself and their daughter—some of it for mourning—and undertook to defend their interest in gauze, lace, and ribbon: "A little of what you call frippery is very necessary towards looking like the rest of the world."

While not overly fond of such objects herself, she was quick to take up the opportunity to invest in the "Small articles" that had "the best profit," including "Gauze, ribbons, feathers, and flowers to make the Ladies gay"; some six months later, when John was at The Hague, she urged him to send black and white gauze and gauze handkerchiefs, wryly adding, "It may not be to the Credit of my country but it is a certain fact, that no articles are so vendible or yeald a greater profit."[23] While Abigail's access to luxury goods changed radically in later years, she maintained a distance from "richness of attire," preferring to dress in an elegant but modest fashion even when appearing in society during John's service as the first American minister to the Court of St. James's and during his later terms as vice president and president of the United States.[24]

Abigail and John Adams were not the only politically prominent couple corresponding between Boston and Philadelphia in the 1770s—and also not the only one concerned with purchasing textiles. John Hancock, John's fellow delegate to the Continental Congress, married Dorothy Quincy in 1775, and both the run-up to that event and the ensuing years involved substantial letter writing and investment in clothing and accessories.[25]

That any textiles survived from John and Dorothy's early years together is remarkable. The separation of war and nation-building wrought even more upheaval for them than it did for the

Adamses, since John Hancock's duties pulled him from city to city. Frequently, Dorothy would remove the household to the new location, arranging the packing and the transportation for herself, her children, and the domestic staff. Even as she "ransack'd" their belongings as John requested, she still preserved, either herself or by placing them in someone else's care, small souvenirs—items that survive today, many cared for now by Revolutionary Spaces and others by the MHS—including small textile fragments, a variety of domestic artifacts, and garments, accessories, and footwear descended through the family.[26]

Two such items in the holdings of the MHS suggest how textiles rich in color and texture could retain their vibrancy as they passed from generation to generation. One extant swatch of silk brocade combines green, silver, peach, and blue in a floral design. Another piece of silk, most likely from a coat that had belonged to John's uncle Thomas Hancock, has now existed for some centuries as a luxurious drawstring purse. The interior—more protected than the exterior over the years—still gives a sense of the gold pattern originally woven into the silk damask. Although the identity of the person who crafted this item is unknown, the pouch appears to date from the late eighteenth or early nineteenth century, as the new republic grew out of the Revolution. As a family keepsake, it may have preserved the memory of the uncle who helped raise John after his own parents passed away; given the timing, it may also have been a memento of John, who died in 1793, as the upheavals of nation-making were still fresh.

Left and below, FIG 3.5: Purse made from silk coat lining. See also Fig. I.8.

Right, FIG 3.6: Swatch of silk brocade probably from a dress, possibly dated as early as the 17th century.

WHILE SOME PATRIOT FAMILIES invested in both domestic and imported goods during the Revolutionary era, the record for William Dawes, Jr. (1745–1799), and his family shows a deliberate and staunch interest in American textile production. Known best as the third horseman on the midnight rides of Paul Revere and William Prescott to Concord in 1775, Dawes was very much a patriot who measured the value of his life's endeavors against the moral worth of goods. This principle also carried into later generations of his family.[27]

Before the famous rides, his contemporaries would have known Dawes, like Revere, as a craftsman and as a powerful voice in Boston's patriot politics.[28] He grew up and apprenticed in Boston as a tanner and leather-worker, and eventually kept a shop in Boston. But the post–Seven Years' War recession and the tariffs imposed on the colonies quickened the political consciousness of Boston's struggling artisans like Dawes. In 1769, he added his name, along with those of notable residents such as Harbottle Dorr, Thomas Greenough, Paul Revere, John Scollay, Ebenezer Storer, and Joseph Warren, to a non-importation agreement that committed the signers to forgo manufactures imported from Great Britain.[29]

On May 3 of the preceding year, Dawes had married Mehitable May (ca. 1751–1793) when he was twenty-three years old and she was seventeen. While we do not know the composition (color, textile, cut, or details) of his outfit that day, an account book from his shop reveals that he had access to ample supplies upon which he could have drawn for his wedding raiment, and

he was not constrained to domestic goods. But we do know, from contemporary newspaper accounts, that he wore a suit of American-woven cloth—that he "dress'd wholly in Manufactures of this Country, wherein he did Honor to himself, and merits the respect of his Province."[30] This was both an early and a strong political statement of the boycott of British goods. Given the conventions of the time regarding citizens of William and Mehitable's class, their marriage would most likely not have appeared in the newspapers at all.

Various notices in the Boston newspapers from 1767 to 1768 hint at new sources that may have helped ardent Whigs express patriotic sentiment without compromising their sense of gentility. As noted above, the advertisement about the Roxbury clothier preparing to manufacture a small quantity of "homespun broad cloth suits" appeared at this time.[31] Given the timing, it is possible Dawes acquired one of the Roxbury suits for his nuptials.

While the ardor with which William Dawes committed to the patriot cause is evident in his acts—the midnight ride, the wedding outfit, the non-importation agreement—that commitment also had a long wake in his family. His

FIG 3.7: Leather pouch, belonging to William Dawes. A modest piece, the bag is offset with neat stitching and a simple cord drawstring. The label reads in part, "This bag contains Sundrey Deeds &c.—& Notes of hand considered of little, or no, Value."

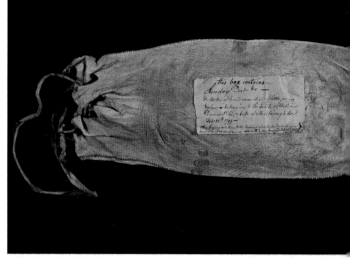

descendants continued to embrace the importance of domestic textile production. The items at the MHS associated with the Dawes family reach from William's Revolutionary generation to the first decades of the nineteenth century, as the early republic took root. The most telling of all these items is an unassuming, monogramed square of blue-and-white checkered cloth, possibly a table covering or neckerchief.

The piece is made of cotton and dyed with indigo.[32] The finished piece is especially light, soft, and flexible. Slubs exist in both the white and blue yarns, confirming it was not commercially made but likely the product of a skilled woman's weaving. That weaver's identity is hinted at in the monogram "LD" embroidered into the upper-left corner of the cloth. Taken together, these details recommend this piece as a product of a family's multi-generational commitment to producing American-made textiles and an example of "homespun" handiwork.

The monogram lifts this ubiquitous textile from obscurity and anonymity.[33] The survival of this simple, vernacular blue-checked square is clearly connected to the Dawes family, even if it is not possible to link it definitively to its maker. In the case of the Dawes family, there are three women with the initials L. D. who could reasonably be assumed to have woven this piece: Dawes's mother, Lydia; his second wife, also Lydia; or his daughter Lucretia. Process of elimination gets us to Lucretia, and the story her

FIG 3.8: Dawes home-spun cloth.

involvement pulls into view is one of national significance.[34]

The best evidence for Lucretia (1788–1855) as the woman behind the monogram is her participation in the home-based textile production business run by her sister Hannah Dawes Newcomb (1769–1851), the eldest daughter of William and Mehitable. Hannah would have come of age during the Revolution—no doubt in a Boston household buzzing with news and gossip related to the patriot cause. Just six years old in 1775, she turned fourteen the year that the Treaty of Paris was signed. In addition to conversations at home, she may have accompanied her father to his shop, where there was apt to be more discussion of ongoing political developments.

Hannah's mature commitment to American textile production is evident in the manuscript records that she left, the earliest of which dates from 1806, after she had married Judge Daniel Newcomb (her second husband) and settled in Keene, New Hampshire.[35] Keene was an early nineteenth-century center of textile production. From Hannah's extant daybooks, a picture emerges of her daily life and household in the dawning years of the young republic. Much of what she chose to record is similar to what we find in journals and diaries authored by both men and women in this era—the mundane, usually beginning with the weather. Hannah's books tell us about her spring cleaning in March and the "yellow" washing of the kitchen; she notes how many candles have been "dipt" on a given day; she records wash days. And she marks changes to her routine: birth, death, sickness, fast days, who has come to tea or when the next dance takes place.

But Hannah also recorded her significant contributions to the family's economic bottom line through what can be described as her "home-shop system" of spinning and weaving. It was common for women, especially outside urban areas, to make linen or cotton cloth for family use or for sale to neighbors or at markets.[36] By the end of the eighteenth century and the start of the nineteenth, homespun cloth was also purchased by the local mills to make men's shirts and coats, aprons, and other items. A largely rural phenomenon, the home-shop system drew upon the labor of multiple family members and/or neighbors to create products in whole or in part. This practice allowed an entire family to take part in "asset" production and accumulation, and diversify the output of the household to meet the family's needs. While there may have been one central skill, generally practiced by a male head of household—such as cordwaining, surveying, or blacksmithing—that characterized a family's "trade," that specialty was augmented through a broad range of other work, including farming, livestock husbandry, cider making, carting, and textile production. Further, home-shop systems opened up opportunities for occasional, often seasonal, work for individuals and households with inconsistent income. The diaries of Martha Ballard of Maine and Samuel Lane of New Hampshire are good comparable examples.[37]

Hannah's journals provide a detailed record of a household deeply involved in this kind of work. She documented the quantities made by, and the payments made to, those working in her shop, as well as the revenues she brought in. Her early nineteenth-century books include plentiful entries with the names of people she employed alongside the kind of work done, the amount of yarn or cloth produced, and the exact compensation she paid them. They provide very concrete data about the economics of home-based textile production, and they also show that Hannah attached a monetary value to the work she and the others contributed, in contrast to what is often overlooked as a woman's invisible contributions to the family balance sheet.

In addition to the local women employed, several relatives also joined in sporadically to spin and weave. Among those, we find her sister Lucretia Dawes, who is listed several times as receiving payment for spinning and weaving. According to the diaries, Lucretia spent ample time in Keene, coming up from Boston on the stage. She weathered severe illnesses in her sister's home, and she ultimately was buried in the cemetery in Keene, in the same plot as her sister and brother-in-law. Other than her appearance in her sister's diaries, and the blue-and-white checked cloth, we know little of her, primarily that she never married and appears to have led a quiet life.[38]

While we may never be able to establish with complete certainty which L. D. created this cotton piece, it nevertheless illustrates one family's multi-generational commitment to supporting the creation of American textiles. Further, succeeding generations of the Dawes family clearly felt this piece of modest work was important enough to preserve and pass on—as important as a silk muff, Chinese export plates, William Dawes's leather document pouch, and other items at the MHS that carry the sort of value more typically recognized as worthy of preservation.[39]

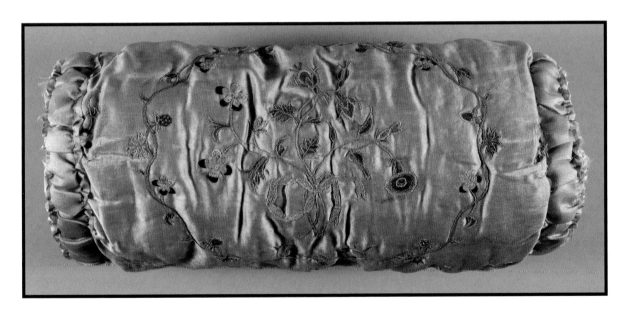

FIG 3.9: An embroidered silk muff believed to have belonged to Hannah Dawes. The seams and casual construction details, seen particularly at each end, indicate that it was likely refashioned from an earlier garment. It may have been a "practice piece" for Hannah or one of her sisters. Although the silk thread embroidery is well done, it does not appear to be professional. Muffs of similar shape, detail, and style were popular during the last quarter of the eighteenth century.

Following page spread:

FIG 3.10: Fabric from an 18th-century dress belonging to Elizabeth Pierpont (later Cunningham).

FIG 3.11: Detail of a 19th-century silk scarf, Hartwell-Clark family.

Piece of Rachael's Grandmother Clark's wedding gown.

16 Russell Avenue,
Watertown, Mass.

Dear Hilda,
This comes to
tell you that I love you and
every day long to see you, and
because it is Christmas I
send you this little quilt
which your great-grand-
mother Clark made for
your mother when she was

19TH-CENTURY NEW ENGLAND
WOMEN AT HOME AND ABROAD

MONG THE TREASURES that reside at the Massachusetts Historical Society there hangs James Brown Marston's expansive, vivid depiction of the State House in Boston in 1801 (see Fig. 4.2a).[1] At that time, many viewers could still recall how the site had served in the Revolution as the setting for both the infamous Boston Massacre on March 5, 1770, and the public reading of the Proclamation of Peace from the State House balcony in April 1783, which marked the end of the war between Britain and the United States. In 1801, the events of the nation's founding had just passed another point of closure when President Washington succumbed to illness in December 1799, the national mourning subsiding as Massachusetts made its passage from its Puritan and Revolutionary trappings into a new century. Marston's composition specifically brings Boston into the new century; it presents a modern metropolis at the dawn of a jaunty new age of uncompromising commerce and consumption.

The canvas frames an intersection of roads under the balcony of the State House, a scene of bustling streets featuring elegant shoppers, vibrant storefronts, and a full public carriage. Marston enriched the image with an abundance of precise details, including signs for actual businesses and vignettes of the types of work that engaged various members of the citizenry. The careful observer may note considerable exactitude in the illustration of ordinary people going about their everyday lives.

Indeed, Marston assembled each person's costume very particularly—and dressed many of them in the latest styles. Several women walk along in feathered hats, the dresses are monochromatic and high-waisted, reticules (small hand-held purses) are in evidence, and the shoes are flat or low heeled. We can see, in the lower-left corner, a woman dressed in exemplary 1801 fashion: her blue overdress, possibly a lighter outerwear coat called a *pelisse*, gives us a glimpse of her white petticoat and a high-waisted bodice with a ruffled, square-shaped neckline. This on-trend pedestrian also possesses stylish accessories, including a parasol, a shawl, and a hat with two plumes jutting out; she walks in flat shoes with pointed toes and bows. Just in front

Facing page, FIG 4.1a: Lap quilt, 1868, with a portrait of Rachel Smith Bagley Clark and letter from Ella Hartwell to Hilda Pfeiffer, her granddaughter.

of her on the street is a similarly attired woman, carrying what is perhaps a handkerchief or fichu or reticule, sporting at least two feathers on her head, and wearing a dress with a low-cut square neckline and a high waist. Gone are the richly patterned dresses with side hoops, panniers, and bum and hip rolls, and so, too, are the heeled shoes. The gentlemen are just as fashionably outfitted, with snug-fitting breeches, high-cut frock coats, shorter waistcoats, and tall hats.

We see, also, a stark contrast between the fashionably dressed individuals and the people who are carting or selling goods and who wear everyday work clothes. The garments of two of these figures, a tall man in the lower-left quadrant of the canvas and a seated woman surrounded by baskets on the right side, have also been rendered with such detail that they are recognizable as the garb of an older generation. He is clad in a long coat that covers much of his form, and the buttons and embroidery also speak to an earlier era. The poof of an old-fashioned wig appears under the side of his hat, possibly a tricorn like Henry Bromfield wore. The woman's dress is a modest and simple item with no suggestion of current style, even decidedly unstylish with its drab color and well-covered neckline. Her head cover has little shape to it, not a hat but a mobcap, only some trimming around its edge but of course no feathers.[2]

The conjunction of the two kinds of clothing—the au courant and the old-fashioned—in this scene shows the reality of how styles overlapped. It captures a particular moment of tran-

sition from the eighteenth century to the nineteenth, and that overlap illustrates an important aspect of how we look at historical self-fashioning: rather than considering someone's choices over a lifetime of changing circumstances and preferences, we freeze them at one moment in time. One thing we can identify with a broader view are people, like Henry Bromfield, who actually persisted in one era's style in subsequent decades, doggedly or more subtly, by favoring more muted versions of newer trends.

In this light, Abigail Adams is an ideal figure through which to explore the sartorial culture of America as the country segued from its Rev-olutionary activities to the creation of a new republic. She was a connected and prominent figure in the closing decade of the eighteenth century, as her husband served first as vice president (1789–1797) and then as president (1797–1801). Mature and practical, she persisted in some "old-fashioned" judgments and options (see her pocket, discussed below) when it came to clothing, but she also understood that the young nation needed to be seen as modern and cosmopolitan. This, for her, created a bit of a conflict when it came to the fashion in American women's attire at the advent of the nineteenth century.

The prevailing trend in women's clothing partook of the same neoclassicism then shaping fine and decorative arts across Western Europe, where motifs adapted from the classical world dominated design trends in architecture and furniture as well as textiles.[3] In the United States, where the Constitution had been in effect for less than a decade when John Adams became president in 1797, neoclassicism served as an homage to the principles of democracy that many Americans believed derived from the ancient republics of Greece and Rome. In general, the emphasis on clean lines, symmetry, and forthright geometry seemed—to some—an appropriate expression of the rejection of monarchy and aristocracy for a system of republican self-governance.

The dresses depicted on Greco-Roman artifacts, such as statuary and ceramics, became the model for women's fashions, effecting a sharp turn away from the silhouette that had been evolving throughout the preceding century. Rather than a very structured form, padded with layers of fabric and profusely ornamented, the neoclassical robe appeared to be a light and supple bit of drapery, with no shape of its own but only that lent by the body of the wearer, with just a touch of cinching between the bust and the waist.

As much as this style purported to allude to the revered democratic-republican cultures of Greece and Rome, it did not necessarily find favor in the eyes of men and women who had imagined the new nation as a republic of virtue. In fact, during John Adams's presidency, when Abigail hosted social gatherings in the presidential home—then located in Philadelphia—she found much to criticize in this "stile of dress." Writing to her sister Mary Smith Cranch in March 1800, she deemed it "an outrage upon all decency" and proceeded to relate how "it has appeared even at the drawing Room":

> a sattin peticoat of certainly not more than three breadths gored at the top, nothing beneath but a chimise over this thin coat, a Muslin sometimes, Sometimes a crape made so strait before as perfectly to show the whole form, the arm naked almost to the shoulder and without Stays or Bodice a tight girdle round the waist, and the "rich Luxurience of naturs Charms" without a hankerchief fully displayd.[4]

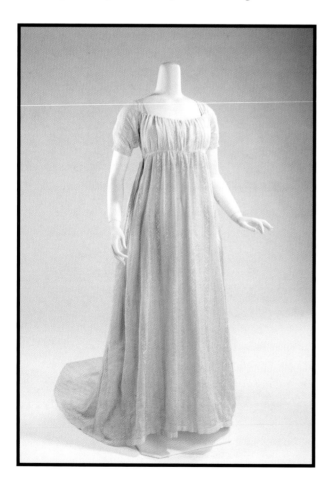

FIG 4.3: Empire silhouette dress, 1800–1805. Courtesy Metropolitan Museum of Art.

Facing page, FIG 4.4: Elizabeth Price memorandum book, 1804.

Fashionable Dresses of the Year

Continuing with a description of one youthful visitor, Adams noted that "when this Lady has been led up to Make her curtzey which she does most gracefully it is true—every Eye in the Room has been fixd upon her, and you might literally see through her." Regarding "the other Ladies," she conceded, "I cannot accuse them of Such departures from female decorum," but she could still contend that "most of them wear their Cloaths too scant upon the body & too full upon the Bosom for my fancy; not content with the *show* which nature bestows; they borrow from art, and litterally look like Nursing Mothers—to Disguise the Strait appearence of the Gowns before, those Aprons, which you say look like fig leaves, were adopted." In a letter composed a month later, Adams qualified her otherwise positive opinion of a young woman with a "la-ment, that the uncoverd bosom should display, what ought to have been veild, or that the well turnd, and finely proportiond form, Should not have been less conspicuous in the dance, from the thin drapery which coverd it. I wishd that more had been left to the imagination, and less to the Eye."[5]

In the March 15 letter, Adams also dropped a comment undermining the notion that neoclassical dresses simply allowed the natural body to shape the cloth: "not content with the show which nature bestows; they borrow from art." Although the style dispensed with so many of the shaping garments that were essential to women's fashion in the eighteenth century, stays (sometimes padded) were employed to boost and shape the bosom, thus contributing to the apparently scandalous effect of the often low-cut neckline of the

FIG 4.5: Dress Abigail Adams appears to have worn in her portrait by Gilbert Stuart. Adams National Historical Park. Image courtesy author.

also made choices in her self-fashioning that acknowledged the importance of being in mode. This awareness is evident in her portrait (1800/1815) by Gilbert Stuart, among the most sought-after American portraitists of that generation, where she appears to demonstrate how a mature woman could wear a neoclassical garment with utmost decorum. From what we can see of her attire as depicted, her dress suggests the popular silhouette of the time, with the high waist, low-cut square neckline, and fitted sleeves. Fortunately, the actual garment has survived, making it possible to confirm how her dress met the dominant style and also where it diverged, even despite apparent later alterations.[6] So we know that, rather than a lightweight cotton, Adams chose a heavier fabric, a high-quality silk, dyed a bronzed plum color. For the sitting, she accessorized the low neckline of the bodice with a high-necked, ruffled chemisette, also known as a "modesty" cloth, more than fulfilling the function of the "hankerchief" mentioned in her letter to her sister. This and other white accessories in the painting play nicely against the purple-hued silk: a light lace fichu drapes her shoulders and a lace bonnet covers her head. Abigail's delicate head cover references the heyday of the stylish mobcap, a world away from the same item on the saleswoman in the Marston painting. The viewer has little sense of how Abigail's hair is styled in the portrait, with the exception of the ringlets framing her face—those curls also a reference to Greek statues. In short, her self-fashioning reveals that she was well aware of what was in style. Was she perhaps also using her portrait as an "instruction" guide for appropriate dress for an American woman in the early republic? Or perhaps to demonstrate to the viewer the attire of a mature woman?

dresses. Like the look that preceded it, and like the look that would follow, the neoclassical gown used art in pursuit of a specific female presentation dictated by a prevailing style.

Despite her misgivings about the diaphanous and potentially revealing gowns, Abigail Adams

4.6: Abigail Smith Adams by Gilbert Stuart, 1800/1815. Courtesy National Gallery of Art.

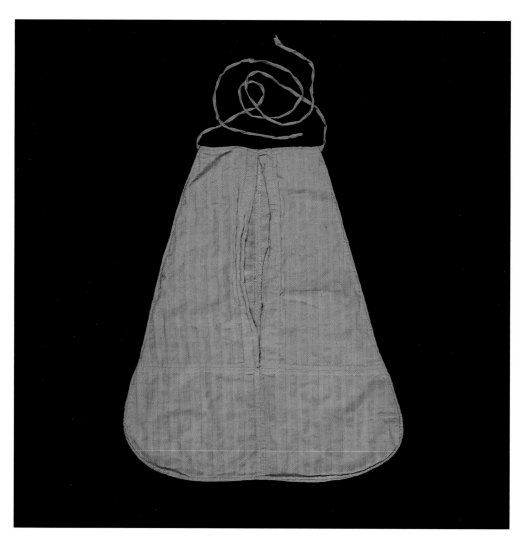

Above, FIG 4.7: Pocket belonging to Abigail Adams, [late 18th–19th century].

Right, FIG 4.8: Elizabeth Coombs Adams's note on Abigail Adams's pocket, before 1903.

Dimity pocket worn
for 50 years (probably) by
Mrs Abigail Adams my
Grand Mother & wife of
John Adams —
all old ladies wore
these under pockets & carried
their keys in them —

With its body-skimming aspect, the fit of these neoclassical dresses not only eschewed the decorum Adams valued but also made impossible one of the most utilitarian items that many women of her generation depended upon: the pocket. The high waist and loose drape of the skirts on these dresses, combined with sheer or semi-sheer fabrics—light cottons, muslins, and silks—left little room for stashing a pocket, which was then a separate item, not sewn into a garment but tied with string or ribbon around a woman's waist and concealed beneath hoops and petticoats. As a consequence, women who favored neoclassical shifts found pockets inconvenient and instead began to carry the type of small purses seen in Marston's painting of State Street.

With regard to her pocket, as with her self-presentation and opinions about new styles, Adams may have had more in common with the man and woman who appear in that painting in their old-fashioned garb than she did with the fashionable people who surround them. Adams opted to continue using the traditional pockets, a choice she likely shared with Martha Washington and other women of their generation.[7] One of Adams's pockets has survived the centuries, passed down in the family, and is now in the textile holdings of the MHS.[8] Fourteen inches long, it is constructed of eight pieces of white dimity cotton, lightweight and woven so as to create raised stripes; cotton tape serves as ties. Dimity was then a recent innovation, the result of "advances in chemical bleaching and soaps of the late eighteenth and early nineteenth centuries," according to historians Barbara Burman and Ariane Fennetaux. They have further noted that "Dimities for pockets, excelling in use and fitting most budgets, demonstrate the transformations in science, industry and technology benefitting consumers across all social ranks."[9]

Its very simplicity and functionality render Adams's pocket so striking. There is no excess, nothing that is not needed for its intended use. Although the maker is unknown, the use of dimity, as Burman and Fennetaux's research suggests, dates it to the closing decade of the eighteenth century or early in the nineteenth. Either way, a manuscript note from Elizabeth Coombs Adams (1808–1903), one of Abigail's granddaughters, confirms that the pocket itself seemed old-fashioned to someone of her generation: "All the old ladies wore these under pockets and carried their keys in them."[10] Burman and Fennetaux elaborate on this common utterance in their concluding chapter, titled with the quotation "This is the sort of pocket our great grandmothers used to wear."

Although Abigail Adams did not avidly embrace the neoclassical frocks adopted by many younger women at the beginning of the nineteenth century, the style of her pocket may have been influenced by the same aesthetic. Simple and unadorned, it shows a shift away from embellished and decorative examples associated with earlier fashions. Whether Adams's pocket owed its straightforward design to prevailing neoclassical principles or to the no-nonsense New England frugality of its owner, it stands in rather sharp contrast to the ornate, frequently colorful pockets made around the same time and in previous decades. Indeed, pockets have a long history, documented in archival records and in the survival of richly embroidered and printed pockets that would have been functional for the wearer while also conveying her stylish sensibility and, if desired, her economic status.[11]

The use of these roomy pockets crossed boundaries of wealth and privilege: a woman of any class was likely to have one present on her person or among her effects. As a manager of

her household economy and her farm, especially during her husband's frequent absences, Adams likely made use of pockets as repositories for papers, small tools, and the like, as did female shopkeepers, domestic servants, and members of the artisan and working classes.[12] According to *Eighteen Maxims of Neatness and Order*, written by "Theresa Tidy" in 1819, the essential contents included "a thimble, a pincushion, a pencil, a knife and a pair of scissors, which will not only be an inexpressible source of comfort and independence, by removing the necessity of borrowing, but will secure the privilege of not lending these indispensable articles."[13] For a house or kitchen maid, living and working in close quarters, a pocket (or possibly pockets) might consti-

Top, FIG 4.9: Pocket, ca. 1784. Courtesy Metropolitan Museum of Art.

FIG 4.10: Reticule or purse, 1840, belonging to the Leverett family and embroidered by Harriet Leverett. Many 19th-century women came to view the reticule as a more fashionable item than its predecessor, the pocket.

Facing page, FIG 4.11: Dress with gigot sleeves, 1832–1835. Courtesy Metropolitan Museum of Art.

tute her only personal space and safely hold her worldly goods: coins, mementos, a bit of ribbon, a lock of hair, a note or letter, a pair of scissors, a piece of bread. Their functionality independent of a garment allowed for items to be carried and concealed without disrupting the line of a dress, so long as that dress was not a sheath of fine fabric.

As POPULAR AS the body-skimming neoclassical figure was, it passed out of fashion in the first decades of the nineteenth century, giving way to a series of new, very structured silhouettes that came to dominate the century, culminating in the "S-curve" that smoothed the transition into the twentieth century.[14] An early stop on the path from forest nymph shift to Victorian structure was the Romantic style that became prevalent in the 1830s, when dresses subtly morphed into more rounded shapes. The waistline migrated back to the actual waist, the neckline contracted a bit, and the small puff sleeves of the neoclassical dress filled out to the classic "leg-of-mutton" sleeve, ballooning at the top of the arm but very close fitting elsewhere. The circumference of the skirt expanded, taking on a modest bell shape, but remaining in reasonable proximity to the lower body. And although the hem descended, it often still left the ankles visible.

A pale green day dress at the MHS carries traces of this transition. The garment's form and style hail from just over a decade after Abigail Adams's death in 1818, showing the move away from the clean lines of neoclassicism toward something more effervescent and Romantic. The work of the garment indicates the hand of a skilled dressmaker, and its presence at the MHS suggests that it most likely has a New England connection, although no information remains about who owned it before its arrival at the

FIG 4.12: Dress with pelerine cape, 1830s.

MHS. Examination by costume historian and mannequin maker Astrida Schaeffer suggests the possibility that the original circa 1830s day dress started out with popular puff sleeves, which were subsequently and painstakingly remade for the 1840s. There have also been changes made in the bodice, indicating it may have been used for maternity wear. The addition of a matching ruffled shawl completed the ensemble, and one can imagine a woman proudly displaying this outfit for a promenade along one of Boston's fashionable thoroughfares.

From the 1840s onward, the desirable line of the torso for dresses would lengthen and shorten in intervals, aided by different corset constructions that stopped at or pulled down past the waist, creating an hourglass figure that emphasized bust and hips in contrast to a small waist. By the 1860s, American women had adopted the full-fledged Victorian aesthetic, the century's most recognized silhouette. With heavier fabrics, often in layers, and shaping undergarments, the Victorian bodice and skirts presented volume extraordinaire. From the shoulders down to the hips, corsets created a breadth across the chest and, from a side view, a forward emphasis to the upper body. The bell-shaped skirt of the antebellum era gave way to an oval that was more snug in front and on the sides, emphasis shifted instead to the rear with the de rigueur bustle. From there, these typically long skirts may have trailed in waves of fabric. The Victorian style in the decorative arts—architecture and interior design as well as fashion—reveled in abundance and embellishment.[15]

The general silhouette from the side foreshadowed the curve that would dominate high-end fashion as the nineteenth century transitioned into the twentieth. Maintaining the top-forward, bottom-backward momentum of the high Victorian figure, turn-of-the-century garments accentuated that shape while slimming it down, as the popular mindset began to reject the aggressively structuring mechanics of nineteenth-century undergarments. Albeit more streamlined, and allowing for more close-fitting dresses, corsets still determined the shape of a fashionable woman's carriage—advancing prow first, her torso and head forward, creating the subtle "S-curve" that exemplified chic mode of the era.

As the styles changed over the course of the nineteenth century, so too did the methods of manufacture and trends in consumption. Most powerful among the forces effecting these changes was a domestic industrial revolution, which sprang from and eclipsed the kind of patriotic fervor for homegrown textile creation that the Dawes family practiced. Indeed, during those same decades, entrepreneurs tried out new textile processing methods in North America, including the Hartford Woolen Manufactory that sent cloth to George Washington and—far better known—Samuel Slater's cotton yarn mill in Rhode Island in the 1790s. Two decades after those experiments, Francis Cabot Lowell and his partners would establish a textile mill along the Charles River in Waltham, Massachusetts, a fully modernized, mechanized operation based on the manufacturing methods that Lowell had observed during a long sojourn in England and the continent. After Lowell's death in 1817, the remaining partners created the Massachusetts mill town named for him, the legacy of which still epitomizes the success of the nineteenth-century New England textile industry. Lowell's integrated factory system and company-town paternalism established the region as the beating heart, or power loom, of domestic mass-production of inexpensive clothing and the American textile business.[16]

Deeply intertwined with the industrial revolution, in America and England, was the cotton revolution that started in the eighteenth century and exploded in the nineteenth, especially in the United States. This abundance was a marked turnaround from the limited availability of cotton in early colonial America, where the absence of an established infrastructure for gathering and spinning this valuable resource kept it scarce. Instead, most cotton textiles used in the colonies through the eighteenth century were imported from England, having originated in India.[17] In England, however, the revolution had begun already—and had a consequent impact on costume. "Nothing," according to historian John Styles, "did more to change the way ordinary people dressed in the eighteenth century than the advent of cotton fabrics." Its effect was pervasive, as "an ever expanding range of textiles made wholly or partly from cotton challenged the supremacy of woollens, silks, linens and leather as materials for waistcoats and breeches, gowns and petticoats, handkerchiefs and stockings." Indeed, the ubiquity of the diaphanous muslin dancing gown that so alarmed Abigail Adams depended upon this change.[18]

Styles has also neatly articulated the line from new technology to dramatic changes in consumption: "New factories powered by water or steam that multiplied from the 1770s housed machines invented specifically to process cotton. From their gates poured forth hank upon hank of machine-spun cotton yarn, and later, especially from the 1820s, yard upon yard of machine-woven cotton cloth, at cheaper and cheaper prices. As prices fell, demand expanded."[19] By the middle of the nineteenth century, the United States had not only embarked on its own cotton revolution—it had become an indispensable exporter of cotton across the Atlantic, including to Great Britain. The demand for cotton grown in the American South drove wealth expansion across the nation—and depended on the forced labor of over a million enslaved people.[20]

The country's thriving cotton economy also benefitted the New England mills—of which there were nearly five hundred in 1860—entwining the region's textile boom with the enslavement economy of the South. Business from Northern mills enriched and sustained Southern plantations, which had supplied New England factories with more than 100 million pounds of cotton as early as the 1830s.[21] Earlier in the century, few white New Englanders would have been likely to recognize their connection to the people held in bondage on cotton plantations, except perhaps Connecticut-born Eli Whitney, whose invention of the cotton gin—an engine that rapidly deseeded cotton fiber—in the early 1790s precipitated the expansion of cotton and enslavement across the lower South.

In the decades preceding the Civil War, however, as antislavery and especially abolitionist movements became highly visible, it would be much harder not to see the connection between enslavement and the quality of life that New Englanders could enjoy due to thriving textile mills—which relied on free rather than enslaved labor and made inexpensive, quality cloth available. In the early 1850s, the enormous success of the abolitionist novel *Uncle Tom's Cabin*, by Connecticut author Harriet Beecher Stowe, would have made it nearly impossible for any literate American not to confront graphic depictions of the exploitations of enslavement.[22] Even as antislavery movements won more support among Northerners in the decades before the Civil War, cotton continued to be *the* textile of production and consumption.

FIG 4.13: Merrimack prints, with fabric samples, [185-].

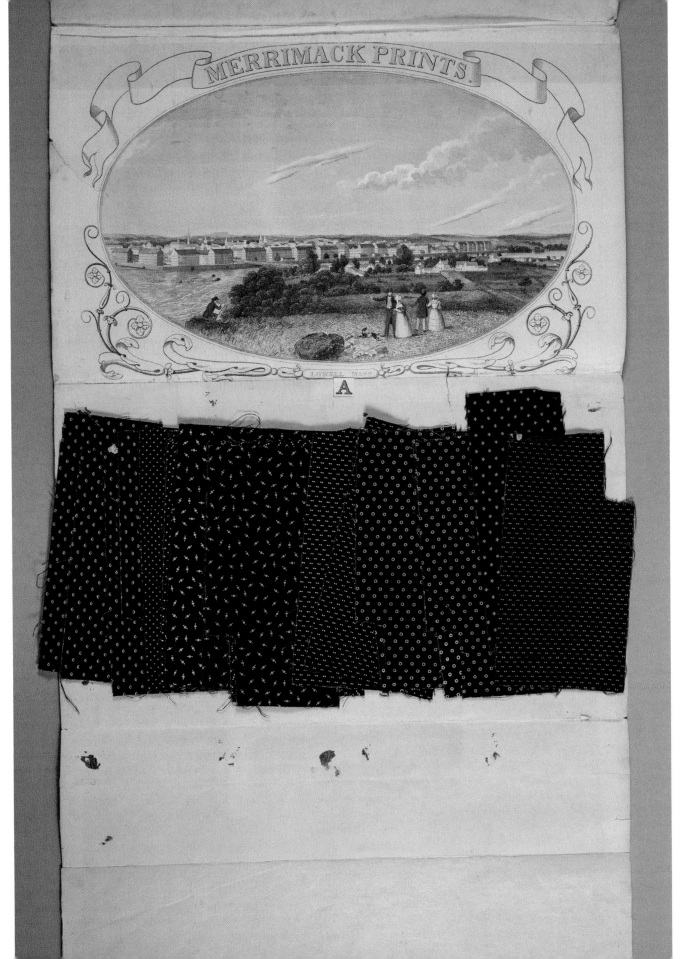

Similarly, while the events and outcomes of the Civil War substantially altered American life, in New England the liveliness of fashion trends during the nineteenth century continued unabated. By lowering the cost of goods and by putting more disposable income into the pockets of working women and men, textile mills shaped the economy of fashion. Both middle- and working-class New Englanders experienced a newfound ability to acquire stylish garments and decorative items that would once have been accessible only to people with much deeper pockets. Women or their dressmakers could purchase cloth at local merchants and dry goods stores and either make up the garments at home or have them created at a shop.[23] Along with American-made goods, shoppers could order European silks and laces, buttons, ribbons, and bows—many also much more affordable than they had been for previous generations. Conversely, as the access to new trends that had once betokened wealth became more accessible on the American market, other items that remained hard to acquire became key expressions of status for the wealthy. As

the century progressed, consumers who could mix high-quality imports into their wardrobe continued to do so.

This dynamic is well represented by two collections of family textiles extant at the MHS, one of which illustrates the earlier decades of the nineteenth century, and the other, the later decades. The Leveretts of the Leverett-Tuttle family of New Hampshire we have seen before, as patriarch Thomas H. Leverett of the town of Keene was a direct descendant of his seventeenth-century progenitors, Gov. John Leverett of the buff coat and Hannah Hudson Leverett of the elusive petticoat. The other, the Hartwell-Clark family, cuts a figure more familiar to our own era, presenting the modern sensibilities of late nineteenth-century women and their fin de siècle clothes.

In the 1830s and 1840s, a close-knit group of women of the Leverett family in New Hampshire produced a variety of garments that convey their skill with the needle and their commitment to family connections. This assemblage of handworked items—such as stockings, baby caps,

and shirts—also speaks to the lingering interest among well-to-do women in creating high-quality needlework projects, despite growing access to premade fashions. Throughout New England, many households produced handmade laces for mantillas, handkerchiefs, shawls, christening caps, and gowns for special occasions and loved ones, and quilted and embroidered textiles used for bonnets, bedcovers, and baby blankets.

The Leverett items now held by the MHS come primarily from the hands of Harriet B. (Nelson) Leverett (1815–1840) and her sisters-in-law Car-oline Hallam Leverett and Harriet Leverett.[24] The earliest items from this group are a pair of stockings and a pair of socks that Harriet Nelson prepared for her April 7, 1834, wedding to Thomas H. Leverett, the John Leverett descendent who ended up in Keene, New Hampshire.[25] The first, for herself, and the second, for her groom. Beginning with machine-knit silk stockings from Europe, the bride-to-be then lavishly hand-embroidered them with French knots and drawn work; the others were plain silk socks to which she added a precise but subtle design at the ankle.

Facing page, FIG 4.14:
Stockings embellished by
Harriet Nelson, ca. 1834.

FIG 4.15: Socks for
Thomas H. Leverett.

The creation of these as wedding attire, as well as their careful preservation by the family, suggests the value that imbued each of the components—the imported, machine-made textile and the skillful needlework of the young lady.

The items attributed to Thomas's sisters Caroline and Harriet were all created for Harriet Nelson Leverett's daughter, Sarah Dutton Leverett (later Tuttle) (1835–1914), and provide a bit of a road map through episodes in Sarah's life.[26] Among these are ten items stitched for Sarah when she was a child, primarily caps, shirts, and dresses. Among the items made for her in 1840, the year her mother died, is a black silk bodice and sleeve from her childhood mourning dress, cut and sewn by either her aunt Caroline or her aunt Harriet, per family records.[27] The sleeve and bodice reflect the style of the era, the bodice close-fitting and the sleeve with the characteristic ballooning between the snug shoulder cap and wrist.

The collection enables today's visitor to have a glimpse of Sarah's social life and her marriage through two shoes, each one extant from a separate pair. The first, for her wedding with Reuben Tuttle of Boston in 1860, features a delicate ribbon and lace rosette; the second, a dancing shoe, is accented with a cheerful pink silk bow. They also show their machine-made origin in the use of the "knock on" heels that replaced the hand-carved wooden heels of earlier generations. Each shoe has a label for Viault-Esté of Paris, a nineteenth-century French

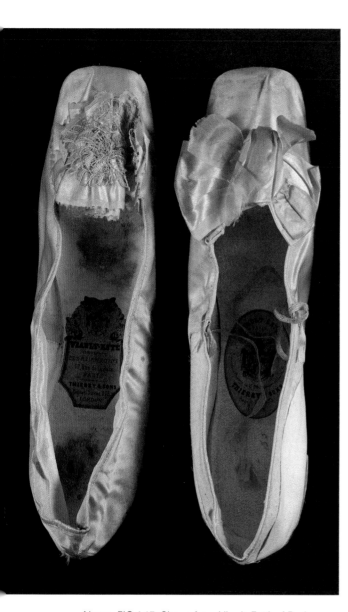

Above, FIG 4.17: Shoes from Viault-Esté of Paris, owned by Sarah Leverett. The shoe on the left was for her 1860 wedding to Reuben Tuttle. The shoe on the right was for dancing.

acing page, FIG 4.16: Bodice
nd sleeve from Sarah Dutton
everett's childhood mourning
ress (front), 1840.

shoe producer, and Thierry & Sons of London, the distributor. This combined business effort was prolific, exemplifying the midcentury success of mass-market production and distribution, but it was also known as high quality. So while Viault-Esté "flooded the American market" in midcentury, the surviving collection of footwear once belonging to Empress Eugénie of France also includes several contemporary pairs with the same label.[28] Among the stories presented here, Sarah Tuttle's shows a particularly dramatic shift in sartorial choices, from the familial bonds expressed in the handmade garments—the work of her beloved aunts—to the appeal of mass-produced shoes, acquired even for a milestone occasion.

The intertwined Hartwell and Clark families also left a rich legacy of textiles with the MHS, a legacy that expresses through dozens of items a similar range of economies of clothing but a more dramatic saga of intergenerational relationships. As described by Anne Bentley, the Society's curator, that history unfolded as the exhibition team teased out the background of the clothing from family letters:

The Hartwell-Clark family papers arrived here with a large wooden trunk full of textiles that seemingly told the story of four very closely knit generations of women of a prominent Watertown family: Rachel Bagley Clark; her daughter Ella Clark Hartwell; Ella's daughter, Rachael Hartwell Pfeiffer; and Rachael's daughter, Hilda Pfeiffer. As we pulled item after item from the depths of the trunk, we marveled at the exquisite handiwork, each with a label that carefully noted who made it and for whom—all the while picturing the family bond they conveyed. Upon reading their letters and diaries, however, we discovered an entirely different story.[29]

Those letters and diaries reveal strife in the Hartwell-Pfeiffer family that turned on the life of Rachael Hartwell (1868–1905), particularly her marriage in 1896 and her death, in childbirth, in 1905. A year after that loss, her widower and her daughter, George (1866–1934) and Hilda Pfeiffer, removed to New York City, and a rift set in between him and his mother-in-law such that Hilda barely knew her Hartwell grandmother, Ella, as she grew up. Ella Hartwell was allowed only very rare contact with Hilda, her only grandchild. During the years they were separated, Ella attempted to send gifts, all of which were apparently returned. The two were able to establish a bond when Hilda returned to Massachusetts to attend college, after which Hilda lived with her grandmother and cared for her during her final illness. It is likely that a number of the Hartwell-Clark treasures now at the MHS passed from Ella to Hilda in this period; many arrived at the MHS with notes pinned to them that appear to be in Hilda's handwriting.[30]

Many of these items evidence, both in textile and on paper, Rachael's lifelong compelling interest in clothing, in appearance generally, and in her own self-presentation. The evidence of this persists in textiles and in documents, each of which augments our understanding of the other. Key among the extant garments, a selection elaborated on below, are an evening ensemble and her wedding dress.[31] Rachael's letters, journals, and what she calls her "journal letters" (long descriptive letters relating the events and impressions of multiple days) establish just how central all attire was to her. Through these records, we see her fascination not only with her own apparel, but with the people around her, sometimes judging how well they present themselves, sometimes intrigued by clothing cultures distant from her own. These textiles and docu-

FIG 4.18: Portrait of Rachael Hartwell Pfeiffer, 1903.

Facing page, FIG 4.19: Bodice of evening gown purchased by Rachael Hartwell, [1892]

ments each augment our understanding of the other and reinforce the opinion of her friends, who all knew her to be fashion conscious and sharply dressed throughout her life.

Over some two decades of correspondence and notebooks written in the United States and abroad, Rachael amassed a vast quantity of observations on the landscape of textiles around her, including the clothing or accessories she bought, admired, and mended; on the garb of people around her, as well as their general attractiveness, or lack thereof; and on her own outfits, both what she wore and what she anticipated. Rachael's correspondence with her parents, Albert and Ella Hartwell, and with her mother in particular, yields frequent references to her wardrobe, in passing reference but also often in considerable detail. Clearly aware of her self-presentation, Rachael selected clothing to shape the impression she wished to make.

This correspondence appears to burgeon, initially, while Rachael was at Wellesley College, from 1887 to 1891, and continues in the ensuing years when she was teaching in Holyoke, Massachusetts. She wrote home often asking for garments or accessories she needed, either for comfort ("I want a clean nightgown more than anything else") or for socializing. In the fall of 1889, Rachael was planning an outfit to wear to a Harvard football game: "I want to wear my new red dress because that is the Harvard color you know—I think you can fix the neck with the crape thin just for once. Will you please freight over and also something to take the place of the green ribbon on my hat. Perhaps Anna will let me take one of her rings & some black ribbon—

I should like to wear your fur cape & a shawl for an extra wrap. You see I shall probably meet a good many people & I want to look my best."[32] Her reports home also included assessments of how well people around her presented themselves. Writing from a summer's holiday at Camp Bemis, Maine, in August 1894, she deemed two daughters of the Long family "homely," noting also that they "wear bloomers"; by contrast, she judged a Mrs. Stuart "a fine looking woman."[33]

According to notes that arrived with Rachael's preserved garments, 1892 constituted a milestone in her economic and self-fashioning agency. Her work as a teacher brought with it a salary that provided a measure of financial independence. Specifically, the cream silk evening dress in that collection had a note pinned to it that identified it thus: "Evening dress belonging to Rachael Hartwell (Pfeiffer) bought with the first money she earned teaching school." Rachael was indeed excited about earning her own money, as she exclaimed in a May 26, 1892, letter to her mother: "Friday I received my first pay I assure you I felt very large—$60! all <u>my</u> own!"

FIG 4.20: Lace shawl. Hartwell family, [18--].

Although the letter itself does not explicate how she spent her bounty, the intersection of the two documents can pinpoint when this gown came into her wardrobe.[34]

The evening ensemble confirms Rachael's fashion sense. A frothy, feminine Belle Époque creation, it would have been a stylish ensemble for a young, unmarried woman in the early 1890s. While the bodice is an effusive affair of white lace, silk, chiffon, and multicolored beads, it is balanced against a simple, minimally designed, but well-tailored skirt, which has a subtle pink stripe running through the silk and a ruffled hem with pink silk peeping out. The hem reflects Rachael's combination of sartorial whimsy and practicality, as the extra bit of silk could have easily been replaced if it became torn or dirty

from skimming the ground. The light-hearted embellishment of the bodice partook of prevailing trends, as noted in an 1894 issue of the *Delineator*: "At present trimmings are used with a profusion that is little short of extravagant," the piece noted. "Frequently a costume is enriched with two or more kinds of garniture, and if the mode of disposal is tasteful, the variety of ornamentation gives no hint of exaggeration. . . . [A] bodice may be adorned with fur, lace, and either ribbon or jet, all of which trimmings are thoroughly congenial."[35]

During this same time period, an entry dated February 14, 1893, in Rachael's journal yields another example of her evening wear choices. On this date, she had attended a College Club reception—possibly for Valentine's Day, given the date. She found the event to be "terribly crowded," leading her to worry that her "beautiful dress would be injured." The description in her journal also underscores Rachael's desire—and ability—to make an impression with her self-presentation: "I was dressed in a beautiful gown of white satin covered with filmy white embroidered chiffon. Indeed I must have been a very pleasing picture." Rachael recorded that she was pleased with impression she made—"I know that I was looking my best, just how well that is I do not know but people looked at me and Mrs Davis wrote me a note afterward in which she said I was charming"—and also that her new beau, George Pfeiffer, had attended.[36]

Rachael had met George in July 1892, when she took a chemistry class at Harvard Summer School—George, with his newly minted doctoral degree, was the instructor. The two began an ambiguous courtship that remained fraught for several years. The initial rockiness seemed to stem from reservations about the match held by both sets of parents and persisted for at least a year. Reflecting generally on the summer of 1893 in her journal, Rachael noted "the progress of my love affair and the adverse position taken by my parents in the matter." Hilda's 1979 narrative of the family history is more pointed: Rachael's parents rejected George as a "foreigner," while George's parents saw her as a mere "'country girl,' a nobody." In the middle of a long April 1893 entry describing the tormenting uncertainty they both experienced at this time, Rachael briefly paraphrased George's gesture toward his conundrum: "He told me that something told him it was wrong for him to kiss me and treat me as he had done, that we were not meant for each other, that I was not to think he did not like me, he did and he wished he could like me better but he could not."[37] Before

the summer, however, George seemed to have overcome whatever stood in his way, and by early May Rachael joyfully declared, "the sun shone once more for me."[38]

While the young couple set aside whatever familial concerns bound them till that spring, they nonetheless did not marry right away. In fact, they did not wed till December 1896, but before that they did something far more alarming to their families: in summer 1896 they set off on a tour of Europe together, entirely unchaperoned. They were not so daring as to travel under the guise of marriage, always securing separate hotel rooms and observing propriety. The effort was stressful, as discussed below, but not so much as to overwhelm how much they enjoyed traveling and one another's company. Indeed, they would spend much of their time abroad in the following years, and of course these adventures presented Rachael with a wealth of opportunities to observe people and their sartorial expression—and to augment her own.

During her travels, Rachael's correspondence with her parents primarily comprised journal letters, a format that provided her room for expansive commentary. Although the couple was usually based in Switzerland and Germany, excursions gave Rachael opportunities for descriptions that moved across cultures and classes. France presented a broad range of tableaux, from haute couture in Paris to the lower-depths of the railway stations. While visiting George's brother Curt in Paris in October 1896, they were able to spend some time at the Continental, "one of the largest, most fashionable and most expensive" of the city's hotels, where Rachael took in this vignette: "In the glass enclosed promenade and waiting room, which surrounds the court, one may see fashion at its very highest; the genuine, much-bedecked, and

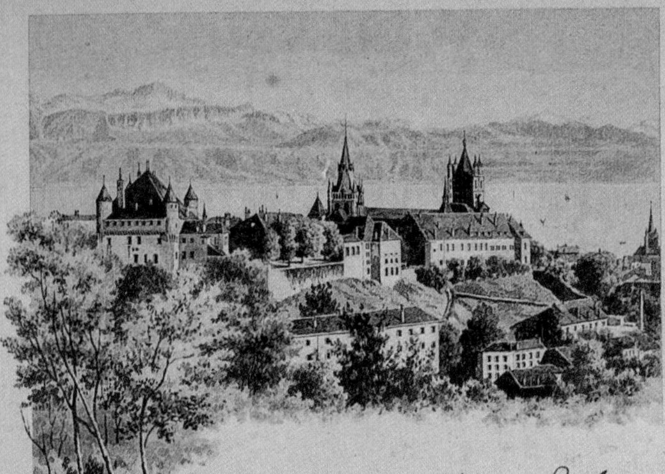

Lausanne Sept 18/96

Dear Pa –

I have ordered two films from Horgan and Robey, finding it impossible to get any of the right kind, here. Please pay the bill which they will send you.

With love to all,

Rachael.

make use of
dia ink blots.
the remain-
not
l. In recalling
ber with
l uesday after-
r with had
gora kitten.
l, but one
e and with
brought in
kittens in a

LAUSANNE 26 IX 96 – 6 EXP LET.

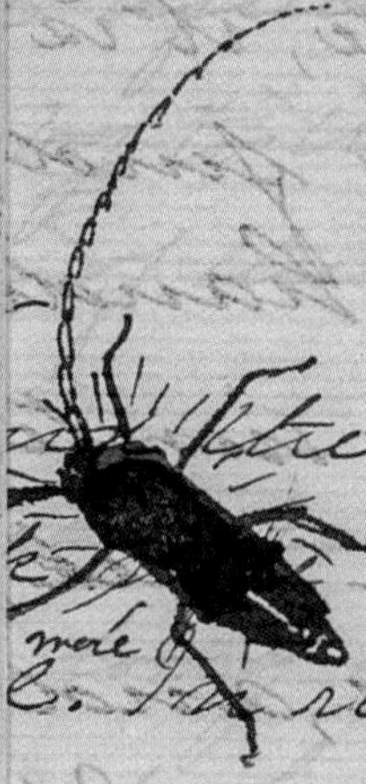

Mr. A. H. Hartwell,
16 Russell Avenue,
Watertown,
Massachusetts,

États-Unis d'Amérique

bepowdered French woman with a tiny waist that looks as though it might at any moment break in two, and the American copy. Occasionally a man goes by with a fashionable poodle at his heels."[39] Her account of the rail trip that took the couple through the countryside to the capital generated very different scenes, in part because they did travel at times in third class, so that they "had the opportunity, moreover, of observing the lower and more characteristically French part of the population." Rachael rendered Hôpitaux Neufs-Jougne, "a railway station seen in a driving rain storm," impressionistically: "A French policeman in a cock hat and great coat on the platform, a lot of dirty country people, also a nun, mounting the train: such was my first impression of France." Later, she depicted the people "lounging about the station. they did not impress us favorably, in comparison with the Swiss. They were common folks, porters and soldiers, but might have been cleaner for all that. Here too stood a woman in wooden sabots, the first I have seen worn."[40]

The following spring, Rachael and George's trip to Milan produced a very different depiction of the local populace in traditional costume. Remarking first on the "great many women in black mantillas, some of lace and some of light knitted wool," Rachael proceeded to describe what "the peasants wore":

> the same bright handkerchiefs on their heads that we see in the fields at home, some had also an elaborate fan-shaped orna-

ment of tin or something like it at the back of the head. . . . On their feet most of them wore little slippers, with soles & little heels of wood leather over the toes and nothing behind. . . . There were also on the streets a great many officals and soldiers in all sorts of uniforms. The high officers wear long capes of black or pale gray a corner of which is thro often thrown over one shoulder. Making them, as they know, look quite picturesque. . . . A convent school went by, the girls in black dress and black hats trimmed with dark blue velvet, guarded by four sisters in black veils.[41]

Along with many records of the fashions around her, Rachael's papers include evidence of how she and George were inspired to indulge in their

FIG 4.22: Sketch of a fishwife, Holland. Rachael Hartwell Pfeiffer, 1899.

own sartorial variation. They sometimes took pleasure in blending in with their surroundings, as they did for a train journey in Switzerland in early 1897: "Not wishing to attract attention in the little country towns we were going to be dressed in our simplest, I in my green woolen, Geo. in an old suit and soft-felt hat, and travelling coat minus the cape. We looked so like ordinary natives, that nobody took much notice of us."[42] Other outfits were less inconspicuous: the fur coat Rachael wore around Zurich earlier that same winter attracted "general attention" and she noted that "it impresses even street car conductors who say good day to me when I have it on, but never notice me in the native jacket." Indeed, the couple also enjoyed impressing their friends on occasion. Invited to dinner at the home of Mrs. Kapp, a family friend, they opted to overdress rather noticeably: "For a joke we thought we would put on full evening dress, George his dress suit and I my pale green silk with low neck. The old lady seemed quite pleased, and the Fahrners stood around and looked their admiration."[43]

As much as George and Rachael enjoyed their adventures together in Europe before they were married, late nineteenth-century conventions made it difficult for them to avoid being perceived as immoral and therefore stigmatized. They apparently always presented themselves honestly as unmarried traveling companions and therefore required separate rooms—and sometimes even ended up at separate hotels.[44] Initially, Rachael appears not to have complained of this often in her letters home—possibly knowing it would just stoke her parents' concern and disapproval—but this began to change as the fall wore on. Early in October 1896, she commented fairly lightly on a woman who was "exceedingly shocked about me, when she first heard who and what we were."[45] A week later, she sent her parents a concise letter—not an entertaining journal letter—presenting a forthright argument for her and George's need to be married as soon as possible, ideally while still in Europe.

Launching into the topic by stating that "It is perfectly clear to me now that I made a very great mistake not to get married last spring," Rachael both reassured her family about the value of the trip and gave an account of the difficulties they encountered:

> We are very glad to be here together and would rather have it so than not to be here at all or to have any third person to interfere with our plans, but we have continually to encounter all sorts of disagreeable things, big and little that detract much from the benefit of the trip. We are kept in a state of continual constant worry and unrest, especially George who has to take the brunt of it all as he manages things. At every hotel there is always the same difficulty in making the proprietor and servants understand. If I wish to meet some nice looking person I have always to refrain, because an explanation would be embarrassing.[46]

The risk of damage to her reputation was clearly a concern, maybe less of an issue with passing acquaintances but very much a concern with regard to George's family: "I am prejudicing George's friends and brothers against me, for although they all treat me with the greatest kindness, I know perfectly well what they are thinking." Suggesting that Albert and Ella have already relented on any earlier qualms about George and now only hold out for a marriage back home, Rachael asked, "What great difference can it make to you whether I am married now or immediately after I get home? You have already made up your mind to that, and I don't think you ought to feel bad to have it come off a few months sooner when it is best for my present and future that it should." Presumably aware of her parents' fear that she may fall into the drama of the woman seduced on a promise of marriage, or the performance of faux ceremony, and then abandoned, she stressed George's integrity: "Don't think that George has suggested this to me. He has done nothing of the kind. It is entirely an expression of my own feelings. He says very little about the matter, but devotes himself to me and my happiness." The letter concludes with a statement that is more imperative than request: "Please send me your consent soon, the sooner the better."

The reply, dated October 25, came from Albert. He presented his and Ella's consent to her plan, albeit with a preamble of his continued cautions against the urgency, if not explicitly the bridegroom himself: "we are very sorry that you seem determined to think that it is best for you to be married at once. I do not see the force of your arguments in favor of your taking such a course. Once you are married, you have given up your freedom, and started on an entirely different life." With a few more lines of hopeless dissuasion, he announced, "Marmie and myself shall not oppose your wishes," and then moved on to advice about the logistics of obtaining a legal and abiding marriage license while abroad.[47] It turned out that on that score at least Albert was right: the bureaucratic obstacles George and Rachael encountered as they tried to marry in Switzerland were too steep, and by late November the couple decided, with a mix of relief and joy, to return to Massachusetts for their wedding, which took place over the Christmas holidays.[48]

Of course, a wedding—especially one at home with family in the holiday season—meant a wedding dress. Once Rachael and George had made the decision to take an American hiatus from their European sojourn in order to get married, Rachael's journal letters began to include regular updates on the dress-making. On November 27, the same day she informed her parents of their change in plans, she shared that, "I am having a white silk gown made which I think will be very beautiful."[49] "I tried my dress on, for the last time, today," she noted on December 8, "and think you will like it"[50] (Fig. 4.23).

Rachael's wedding gown is of a more conservative style than her earlier ensemble, while still showing off the popular S-curve silhouette. The heavy cream silk, with its tone-on-tone embroidery, features a well-fitted bodice and high neck. The full skirt has a slight train. It contrasts with the playful, youthful exuberance of the earlier dress. Rachael chose a London-made, two-piece wedding ensemble (bodice and skirt), purchased from the fashionable and select London textile and garment establishment of Marshall and Snelgrove. The establishment, started in 1838 by John Marshall, had a clientele of elite shoppers by the end of the century; albeit a department store that carried ready-to-wear lines, its in-house couturier workroom allowed customers the extra level of attention and fitting associated with high-quality, exclusive products.[51]

While Rachael and George clearly drew upon desirable shops and capable tradespeople for their attire and accessories, Rachael still maintained her hand at the needlework skills familiar to earlier generations of American women. She regularly set to mending both her and George's clothes during their travels, but her facility with a needle is particularly apparent in the story of a green velvet dress that weaves through her correspondence in the early months of 1897, after she and George have returned to Europe.[52]

The image above shows three dresses on display in the exhibition. Left to right, they are Rachael Hartwell Pfeiffer's wedding dress (Fig. 4.23), Pfeiffer's evening gown (Fig. 4.19), and the dress with pelerine cape (Fig. 4.12).

Facing page, FIG 4.23:
Pfeiffer wedding dress

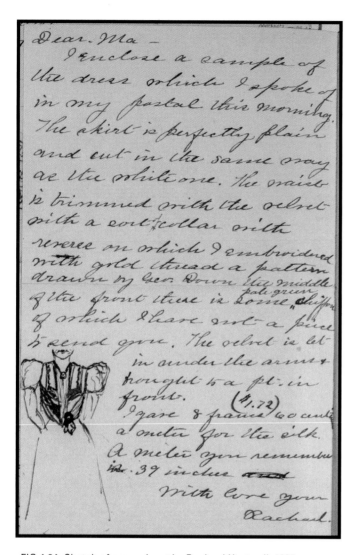

FIG 4.24: Sketch of green dress by Rachael Hartwell, 1897.

I embroidered with gold thread a pattern drawn by Ger. Down the middle of the front there is some pale green chiffon of which I have not a piece to send you. The velvet is let in under the arms & brought to a p(oin)t in front." The letter included a sketch as well, and a sample of the fabric was enclosed with it.[53] She mentioned working the embroidery in several subsequent messages. Finally, in February she was able to announce, "I have spent a large share of my time in the last week getting a new gown made. It was finished and I wore it last night. G. says it is the finest he ever saw. Of course I will tell you all about it in the next letter (dark green silk with ditto velvet)."[54]

The response from home was full of admiration for the fabric and design. Her father replied early in March to say that "Marmie & Jessie, to say nothing of myself, like your dress very much. Kate said, when I showed her the drawing, 'How nice it fits on her.'" A few days later, Ella penned her own note to say, "You knew we should be glad you had the pretty gown, I think the material lovely—so says Bettie, Jessie, Jane, Anna, all endorse it."[55] Rachael's observations about attire, her enthusiasm for fashion and self-fashioning, made up a significant part of her expression and how she shared her life with her loved ones, even as she resided thousands of miles away.

Rachael and George did eventually return to live in the States, but it was a relatively brief reunion for the family. Not yet forty years old, Rachael died as her daughter Hilda was born in 1905. In the many condolences that followed, friends often shared their memories of Rachael's sense of style. "The dresses she wore always looked more picturesque than any body else's," remarked one mourner. Theodora Chase reached out to thank Ella Hartwell for passing on to her Rachael's "dainty dressing sacque": "Ever

While some or most of the dress-making work was likely consigned to a seamstress, Rachael kept for herself the embroidery to embellish it, with a design that George created. Rachael first described the new gown in a letter to her parents dated January 20. "The skirt is perfectly plain and cut in the same way as the white one," she explained. "The waist is trimmed with the velvet and a sort of collar with reverse on which

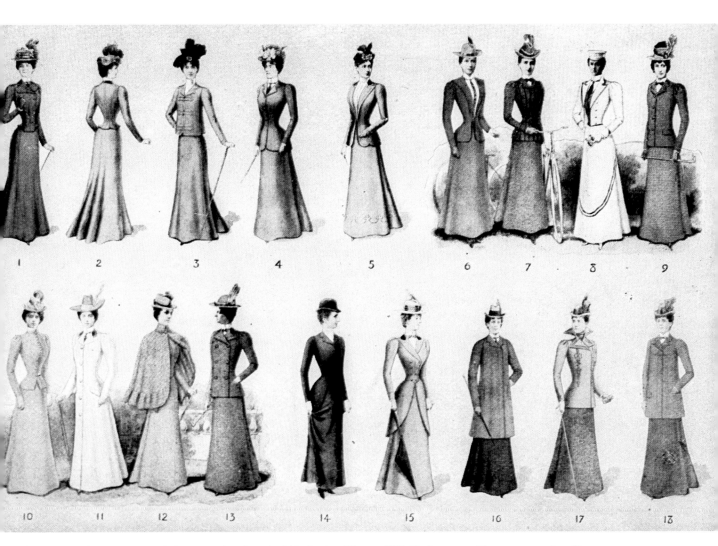

FIG 4.25: This image from a J.A. Dunn catalog, found within Rachael Hartwell Pfeiffer's papers, illustrates popular silhouettes from the turn of the century.

since Sunday I have wanted to thank you for remembering us with something of Rachael's."[56]

One of the most touching survivals from the entwined Hartwell and Pfeiffer families is a lap quilt that Ella Hartwell, Rachael's mother, attempted to send to Hilda as a Christmas gift in 1913, despite the ongoing rift with George (see Fig. 4.1). Hilda's great-grandmother Rachel Clark had made this quilt in about 1868 on the birth of her granddaughter and namesake, Rachael Hartwell. The quilt comprises hundreds of pieces of fabrics from brocaded silks to printed cottons, fragments of clothing belonging to various family members. The pieces of textiles serve as a visual journey through the family history, one piece identified with a note—in Ella Clark's handwriting—pinned to the quilt: "Piece of Rachael's Grandmother Clark's wedding gown." In the letter that Ella wrote to accompany the gift, she told "Dear Hilda,"

> I love you and every day long to see you, and because it is Christmas I send you this little quilt which your great-grand-mother Clark made for your Mother when she was about your age. I hope that you will like to have it over you and that you will care for it as carefully as your dear Mother did.

This charming family record did ultimately find its way to Hilda.

The Leverett-Tuttle and the Hartwell-Clark textile collections share not just a century but also a particular kind of family history—a woman's apparent preservation of the garments, or pieces of garments, that she associated with the mother that she lost very early in life. Many items in the first set arrived with an attached identifying note penned by Sarah Dutton Tuttle. Hilda Pfeiffer's connection to the textile evidence of her mother's life may be less immediately documented, and was possibly interrupted by the family rift, but the care with which the family preserved items from Rachael's life is apparent. Both collections exemplify the way in which old and outdated textiles might be held onto for sentimental, and sometimes practical, reasons and subsequently acquire icon status within the family. Properly cared for and made accessible to a broader audience, they have also become primary sources for historical insight.

FIG 4.1b: Lap quilt, sewn by Rachel Smith Bagley Clark for her granddaughter Rachael Hartwell, 1868. See also FIG 4.1a.

FIGS 4.26a, b (detail): Fan belonging
to Frances Locke Osgood.
Made in France in the early 19th
century, this fan is decorated with
figures wearing attire that evokes
Renaissance lushness, a hallmark of
the Romantic style of the 1830s.

Following page:
FIG B.1: Peace calico, ca. 1865

NOTES

Introduction

1. Max Savelle and Robert Middlekauff, *A History of Colonial America* (New York: Holt, Rinehart, and Winston, 1964), 426. For more scholarship with similar information about wool, see Brett Bannor's "A Republic of Wool: Founding Era Americans' Grand Plans for Sheep," *Journal of the American Revolution*, March 17, 2017, All Things Liberty, https://allthingsliberty.com/2017/03/republic-wool-founding-era-americans-grand-plans-sheep. For cotton, see Giorgio Riello, *Cotton: The Fabric That Made the Modern World* (Cambridge: Cambridge University Press, 2013); and Jonathan Eacott, *Selling Empire: India in the Making of Britain and America, 1600–1830* (Chapel Hill: Omohundro Institute of Early American History and Culture and the University of North Carolina Press, 2016).

2. For information on British textile imports to the American colonies, see R. C. Nash, "South Carolina Indigo, European Textiles, and the British Atlantic Economy in the Eighteenth Century," *Economic History Review*, n.s. 63, no. 2 (2010): 362–392; Stanley Chapman, "British Exports to the U.S.A., 1776–1914: Organisation and Strategy (3) Cottons and Printed Textiles," in *Textiles in Trade: Proceedings of the Textile Society of America Biennial Symposium, September 14–16, 1990, Washington, DC* (Los Angeles: Textile Society of America, 1990), available online at http://digitalcommons.unl.edu/tsaconf/598.

3. For more than half a century, historians have attempted to pin down how colonial Americans understood themselves in relation to England. More specifically, some have sought to explicate the process of Anglicization, as some scholars call it, in colonial America. John H. Murrin, for example, argued that the upper crust of colonial America displayed "a keen desire to recreate British society in America and took pride in the extent to which their societies were becoming increasingly Anglicized." T. H. Breen expanded this idea to other classes as well and argued that a broad colonial consumer revolution began midcentury. According to this data, British merchants unloaded vast amounts of goods onto American markets, and British Americans scooped up chests of tea, boxes of porcelains, reams of cloth, pounds of nails, and more. While clothing may not have featured prominently in much of that scholarship, the two—textiles and self-image—are deeply entwined. See especially John M. Murrin, "The Legal Transformation: The Bench and Bar of Eighteenth Century Massachusetts," in *Colonial America: Essays in Politics and Social Development*, ed. Stanley N. Katz and John M. Murrin (3d ed.; New York, 1983), 540; T. H. Breen, "An Empire of Goods: The Anglicization of Colonial America, 1690–1776," *Journal of British Studies* 25, no. 4, Re-Viewing the Eighteenth Century (1986): 467–499; Phyllis Whitman Hunter, *Purchasing Identity in the Atlantic World: Massachusetts Merchants, 1670–1780* (Ithaca: Cornell University Press, 2001); and Kate Haulman, *The Politics of Fashion in Eighteenth-Century America* (Chapel Hill: University of North Carolina Press, 2011). See also Murrin's dissertation, "Anglicizing an American Colony: The Transformation of Provincial Massachusetts" (Ph.D. diss., Yale University, 1966); Kenneth John Myers, "Reinventing the American Wing: The Detroit Institute of Arts," *American Art* 24, no. 2 (2010): 18–21; and Eliga H. Gould, "A Virtual Nation: Greater Britain and the Imperial Legacy of the American Revolution," *American Historical Review* 104, no. 2 (1999): 476–489.

4. Note that scholars have pointed out that the relationship of cost and global trade in these centuries is more complex than a simple sum of distances traveled. "Available textiles" for the colonial buyer, argues Linda Baumgarten, "were limited more by tariffs and navigation acts than by distance" (*What Clothes Reveal: The Language of Clothing in Colonial and Federal America* [New Haven: Yale University Press, 2012], 76). See also John Styles on the popularity of cotton: *The Dress of the People: Everyday Fashion in Eighteenth-Century England* (New Haven: Yale University Press, 2008), 109.

5. For overviews of silk production and trade, see Mary D. Doering, "Sericulture, 1715–1785," in *Clothing and Fashion: American Fashion from Head to Toe*, ed. José Blanco F., vol. 1: *Pre-Colonial Times through the American Revolution*, ed. Mary D. Doering (San Francisco: ABC-CLIO/Greenwood, 2015), 249–253 (publication cited hereafter as *Clothing and Fashion*, with author and entry title and volume and page number); Melinda Watt, "Textile Production in Europe: Silk, 1600–1800," October 2003, in Heilbrunn Timeline of Art History, The Metropolitan Museum of Art

(2000–), www.metmuseum.org/toah/hd/txt_s/
hd_txt_s.htm; Amelia Peck, ed., *Interwoven Globe: The Worldwide Textile Trade, 1500–1800* (New York: The Metropolitan Museum of Art, 2013); and Lesley Ellis Miller, *Selling Silks: A Merchant's Sample Book* (London: V&A Publishing, 2014).

6. Records held at the Victoria and Albert Museum include many related to the work at Spitalfields, including drawings by noted designers such as Anna Maria Garthwaite.

7. For Virginia silk, see Charles E. Hatch, "Mulberry Trees and Silkworms: Sericulture in Early Virginia," *Virginia Magazine of History and Biography* 65, no. 1 (1957): 3–61; and Lee Pelham Cotton, "Silk Production in the Seventeenth Century," Spring 1996, Historic Jamestowne: Part of Colonial National Historical Park Virginia, National Park Service, U.S. Department of the Interior, https://www.nps.gov/jame/learn/historyculture/silk-production-in-the-seventeenth-century.htm.

8. For Benjamin Franklin and silk production in America, see Nelson Klose, "Sericulture in the United States," *Agricultural History* 37, no. 4 (1963): 225–234; and Ben Marsh, "The Republic's New Clothes: Making Silk in the Antebellum United States," *Agricultural History* 86, no. 4 (2012): 206–234. For Eliza Lucas Pinckney, see Darcy R. Fryer, "The Mind of Eliza Pinckney: An Eighteenth-Century Woman's Construction of Herself," *South Carolina Historical Magazine* 99, no. 3 (1998): 215–237; and Ben Marsh, "A Visitor from South Carolina: Mrs. Eliza Pinckney," in *Enlightened Princesses: Caroline, Augusta, Charlotte, and the Shaping of the Modern World*, ed. Joanna Marschner (New Haven: Yale University Press, 2017). Pinckney family letters are available in *The Papers of Eliza Lucas Pinckney and Harriott Pinckney Horry Digital Edition*, ed. Constance Schulz (Charlottesville: The University of Virginia Press, 2012–2020). In 1975, the *South Carolina Historical Magazine* published "Letters of Eliza Lucas Pinckney, 1768–1782," ed. Elise Pinckney, 76, no. 3 (1975): 143–170, available online at www.jstor.org/stable/27567320.

9. This *American Weekly Mercury* advertisement is the first published mention of calamanco shoes for sale in America that the author has discovered.

10. For information on dyes, see Carmella Padilla and Barbara Anderson, eds., *A Red Like No Other: How Cochineal Colored the World* (New York: Skira Rizzoli, 2015); Sarah Lowengard, *The Creation of Color in Eighteenth Century Europe* (New York: Columbia University Press, 2005); Ed Crews, "Weaving, Spinning, and Dyeing: Dexterity and Detective Work," *CW Journal*, Winter 2007, available on the Colonial Williamsburg website at https://research.colonialwilliamsburg.org/foundation/journal/winter07/weaving.cfm; and Jodi Sietsema, "18th-Century Colors and Dyes," *Courier/NWTA Spy*, Winter 2000, The North West Territory Alliance. For indigo and purple, see Sarah Bond, "The Hidden Labor behind the Luxurious Colors of Purple and Indigo," October 24, 2017, *Hyperallergic*, https://hyperallergic.com. For seventeenth-century color swatches, see Jacob Kastrenakes, "Before Pantone, There Was This Hand-Painted 17th Century Color Guide," May 13, 2014, *The Verge*, www.theverge.com.

11. For more on cochineal red, see Mary Miley Theobald, "Putting the Red in Redcoats," *CW Journal*, Summer 2012, available on the Colonial Williamsburg website at research.colonialwilliamsburg.org/foundation/journal/summer12/dye.cfm.

12. Bernard de Mandeville, *The Fable of the Bees; or, Private Vices, Publick Benefits*, 3d ed. (London: J. Tonson, 1724), 411–413. Also reprinted in Erin Mackie, ed., *The Commerce of Everyday Life: Selections from "The Tatler" and "The Spectator"* (Boston: Bedford/St. Martin's, 1998), 559–560.

13. John Adams to Abigail Adams, October 12, 1782, in *Adams Family Correspondence*, ed. Lyman H. Butterfield et al. (Cambridge: Harvard University Press, 1963–), 5:15 (hereafter *AFC*). All Adams Papers volumes cited hereafter by series title, volume, and page numbers. Almost all of the Adams Papers published volumes, with transcription and annotations, are also available online at the Massachusetts Historical Society in the Adams Papers Digital Edition, www.masshist.org/publications/adams-papers. Correspondence between John and Abigail Adams, and some other items, are also in the Adams Papers Electronic Archive, www.masshist.org/digitaladams, which presents facsimiles of the original manuscripts with transcriptions.

14. James Vincent, advertisement, *New England Weekly Journal*, April 7, 1729, p. 4.

15. Some colors were notorious for fading, such as purple. Writing in her recipe book in 1756, Eliza Pinckney recorded a method for freshening purple: "To

make a Water to Recover faded purple. Take an ounce of Salt of Tartar & put it in a pint of Spring water and Shake it well together; 'tis fit for use emediately." Eliza Lucas Pinckney, receipt book, 1756 (call number 43/2178), South Carolina Historical Society, Charleston.

16. The actual costs of acquiring textiles and the subsequent "making up" into clothing are difficult to ascertain in currency terms understood by modern readers. Rapidly changing supply and demand, based on production and shipping, and economic upheavals resulting from war or new trade alliances all had the potential to impact pricing of raw and finished goods. Conversely, labor costs in early America remained fairly consistent throughout the eighteenth century. For overviews, see Baumgarten, *What Clothes Reveal*; Styles, *The Dress of the People*; Peck, *Interwoven Globe*; Riello, *Cotton*; and Eacott, *Selling Empire*.

17. Scholars producing important research about New England quilts and petticoats include Lynne Z. Bassett, *Massachusetts Quilts: Our Common Wealth* (Lebanon, N.H.: University Press of New England, 2009); Pamela Weeks and Don Beld, *Civil War Quilts* (Atglen, Pa.: Schiffer Pub., 2012); and Baumgarten, mentioned above. Examples of extant petticoats can be found at a number of museums and historical organizations, such as Colonial Williamsburg, the Connecticut Historical Society, Historic Deerfield, and the Metropolitan Museum of Art.

18. For the dress of the cavaliers, see Mary D. Doering's overview, "Cavaliers: 1600–1714," in *Clothing and Fashion*, 1:51–53.

19. Doering, "Cavaliers: 1600–1714," 1:51.

20. A tidy overview of MBC's seventeenth-century sumptuary laws can be found in George Edward Ellis's *The Puritan Age and Rule in the Colony of the Massachusetts Bay, 1629–1685* (Boston: Houghton, Mifflin, 1888), 263–266.

21. This petticoat, discussed further in chapter 1, is in the collection of the Revolutionary Spaces and housed (object number 1910.0050.035) in the Old State House, Boston.

22. For information relevant to Massachusetts and New York, see Massachusetts and New York General Assembly, February 1777, Correspondence on Limiting the Prices of Commodities, in the Thomas Jefferson Papers at the Library of Congress: Series 1: General Correspondence, digital facsimiles available online through the Library of Congress at www.loc.gov/item/mtjbib000239. The first page of this document, dated February 9, 1777, is a letter on the price regulations in Boston. See also *Boston, Feb. 19th, 1777. In Pursuance of the Act of the General Assembly of This State Entitled "An Act to Prevent Monopoly and Oppression,"* [Broadside, Boston, 1777], available online through the Library of Congress at www.loc.gov/item/rbpe.04000900. For an extensive retrospective survey of labor and material costs in Massachusetts, see Carroll Davidson Wright, *Comparative Wages, Prices, and Cost of Living: From the Sixteenth Annual Report of the Massachusetts Bureau of Statistics of Labor, for 1885* (1885; Boston, 1889).

23. *Report of Commissioners on Bureau of Labor Statistics, to the Legislature, June Session, 1872* (Manchester: James M. Campbell, 1872), 18–19. See pages 10 to 22 of this report for a detailed and interesting history of prices in eighteenth-century New Hampshire, along with the cultural forces shaping them.

24. Examples of reuse and repairs of shoes are found in the daybooks of the Pingry family (Salem), the Pope family (Salem), and Col. John Welch (Plaistow, N.H.), all found at the Phillips Library of the Peabody Essex Museum; Col. John Montgomery (Haverhill, N.H.), in the collection of the Haverhill Historical Society; and Samuel Lane (Stratham, N.H.), in the collection of the New Hampshire Historical Society, to name just a few.

25. The Sarah Williams 1738 probate inventory is held by Historic Deerfield, in Deerfield, Massachusetts.

26. For an opportunity to view multiple inventories containing textile valuations, see Abbott Lowell Cummings, *Rural Household Inventories: Establishing the Names, Uses and Furnishings of Rooms in the Colonial New England Home, 1675–1775* (Boston: Society for the Preservation of New England Antiquities, 1964).

27. As noted by Beverly Lemire in "Consumerism in Preindustrial and Early Industrial England: The Trade in Secondhand Clothes," *Journal of British Studies* 27 (1988): 1–24. Among the New England auction houses taking part in this business were those run by Samuel Larkin in Portsmouth, New Hampshire; William Lang in Salem, Massachusetts; and John Gerrish in Boston. For additional information, see the post "Samuel Larkin House," November 23, 2011, on the *Walk Portsmouth* blog, walkportsmouth.blogspot.com/2011/11/samuel-larkin-house.html; Tara Vose

Raiselis, *From the Elegant to the Everyday: 200 Years of Fashion in Northern New England* (Saco, Maine: Saco Museum, 2014), 3; and Kimberly Alexander, "Secondhand Clothes Trade, 1715–1785," in *Clothing and Fashion*, 1:248–249.

28. Robert Campbell, *The London Tradesman* (1747; Newton Abbot, UK: David & Charles Publishers, 1969), 90–94.

29. See Lemire, "Consumerism in Preindustrial and Early Industrial England," p. 5, note 7. See also Alexander's entries "Secondhand Clothes Trade, 1715–1785" and "Slaves and Servants, Runaway Notices for, 1715–1785" in *Clothing and Fashion*.

30. Styles, *The Dress of the People*, 59–60.

31. Notice by David Lyell in the *Boston Newsletter*, July 23, 1716. This and many similar advertisements posted by enslavers have been digitized and made available through *The Geography of Slavery in Virginia*, a website and database created by Tom Costa et al. and hosted by the University of Virginia, http://www2.vcdh.virginia.edu/gos/index.html. See, for example, Robert Pierson's post in the October 8, 1733, issue of the *New-York Gazette* for a "Man, named Jack" who "had on when he went away, a dark brown straight bodied Coat with Brass Buttons, a light coloured Great Coat, Two homespun Tow Shirts, two pairs of Drawers, a pair of orange coloured Stockings and indifferent pair of shoes, a good felt hat."

32. Notice by James Scrosby, *Virginia Gazette*, November 3, 1768.

33. *Boston Gazette*, July 28, 1728.

Chapter 1

1. The surviving piece at the MHS is 4 centimeters by 5 centimeters and housed in a daguerreotype frame. In the process of completing research for the exhibition and book, I was able to ascertain that there are in fact four extant pieces of the textile: at the MHS; at the Radcliffe College archives; at the Pilgrim Monument and Provincetown Museum, Provincetown; and in a private collection. The most detailed examination of the MHS textile fragment was undertaken by MHS curator Anne Bentley and Camille Breeze of Museum Textile Services with assistance from Historic New England.

Prof. Whitney Martinko researched the Radcliffe fragment for an essay written during her undergraduate training at Harvard: "On Damask and Priscilla: The Changing Role of Textiles in the Identity of an American Family," an essay submitted for History 1610 taught by Laurel Thatcher Ulrich and Ivan Gaskell. Per the WorldCat cataloging record (www.worldcat.org/oclc/122386576) for this piece, it "examines the claim that a fabric swatch in the holdings of the Radcliffe Archives was part of the trousseau of Priscilla Mullins Alden (1602–ca. 1680)."

In August 2018, I was able to examine the piece at the Pilgrim Museum, thanks to the assistance of the museum's staff, Deputy Executive Director John DeSouza, and Executive Assistant Diana Batchelor.

A fourth fragment was sold at auction on February 19, 2011, by WorthPoint auctioneers to an unknown purchaser. The piece differs in size and the depth of color. Where the other fragments are roughly square, this piece is 1¾ by 5½ inches. According to the notes with the piece, it was tucked away from light for many years, which may account for the deeper green. However, the wool and the pattern, in combination with the provenance, indicate it is from the same textile. For additional information, see the article "Piece of Mayflower Passenger Priscilla Alden's Dress" at the WorthPoint website: www.worthpoint.com/worthopedia/piece-mayflower-passenger-priscilla-133776355.

2. Today, the fragment appears to be a green-blue, but any plant-, insect-, or animal-based dye is apt to be "fugitive"—a dye that is not color fast and therefore subject to alteration over time. In this piece, the original threads appear to both be blue: a light blue warp and medium blue weft that create the appearance of green. The identification of the material corrects a "linen-damask" identification that had been on record at the MHS. The change stemmed from the examination by Historic New England and Museum Textile Services, referenced above.

3. A transatlantic overview of the Mullins family migration is provided by three museums. Dorking Museum & Heritage Centre, https://www.dorkingmuseum.org.uk, based in Dorking, Surrey, which is where the house in which Priscilla lived prior to taking passage on the *Mayflower* still survives at Nos. 58–61 West Street. The Alden House Historic Site presents useful information about John and Priscilla Alden at its website, www.alden.org, and hosts a house museum in Duxbury, Massachusetts. For more on material culture related to the first English settlers to voyage

to Plymouth, see the website of Pilgrim Hall Museum, www.pilgrimhallmuseum.org. Desirée Mobed, Director of the Alden House Historic Site, and Associate Curator Rebecca Griffin at the Pilgrim Hall Museum assisted with the research for this book.

4. Useful information about cordwainers and the earliest shoemakers to arrive in America can be found at the websites of the Honourable Cordwainers' Company (www.thehcc.org/framelss.htm) and Colonial Williamsburg (www.colonialwilliamsburg.org/locations/shoemaker). Harry Schenawolf provides a useful overview in his article "Cordwainers & Cobblers, Shoemakers in Colonial America," March 8, 2016, on his website *Revolutionary War Journal*, www.revolutionarywarjournal.com/cordwainers. See also, especially, D. A. Saguto, ed. and trans., *M. de Garsault's 1767 Art of the Shoemaker: An Annotated Translation* (Lubbock: Texas Tech University Press, 2009).

5. The first quotation appears in a letter to the Worshipful Company of Cordwainers included in the Huntington Library's first edition of Smith's *Generall Historie of Virginia*. The list of recommended apparel appears on page 161 of the book. John Smith, *The Generall Historie of Virginia, New-England, and the Summer Isles* (London: I.D. and I.H. for Michael Sparkes, 1624).

6. William Wood, *New England's Prospect* (1634; Boston, 1865), 189.

7. Given the activity in shoemaking and tanning in the northern colonies, it is not surprising that the first American guild was that of the "Shoomakers of Boston." Its charter of incorporation was granted by the Massachusetts Bay Colony on October 18, 1648. See John R. Commons, "American Shoemakers, 1648–1895: A Sketch of Industrial Evolution," *Quarterly Journal of Economics* 24 (November 1909): 39–44. A nineteenth-century view of Lynn's history as an epicenter of the American shoemaking industry appears in Alonzo Lewis and James R. Newhall, *History of Lynn* (Boston: John L. Shorey, 1865); reference to "Kertland" on page 154. See also Alexander, "Footwear, 1600–1714," in *Clothing and Fashion*, 1:107–109.

8. For William Mullins's will (proved July 23, 1621, at Dorking, County Surrey, England), see *The New England Historical and Genealogical Register* 42 (January 1888): 62–64.

9. Hannah Hudson emigrated on the *Susan and Ellen* in 1635. Charles Henry Pope, *The Pioneers of Massachusetts, a Descriptive List* (Boston: Charles H. Pope, 1900), 246. For a passenger list, see "Great Migration: Passengers of the *Susan and Ellen*, 1635," at Geni.com: www.geni.com/projects/Great-Migration-Passengers-of-the-Susan-and-Ellen-1635/people/15966.

10. The note is part of the MHS Collections Files, Textiles—Needlework Misc. 010.

11. For details of John Leverett's life, see the finding aid for the Leverett papers at the MHS and Charles Edward Leverett, *A Memoir Biographical and Genealogical, of Sir John Leverett, Knt., Governor of Massachusetts, 1673–79* (Boston: Crosby, Nichols and Company, 1856).

12. Many useful sources are now available on the history of petticoats. See, for example, Bassett, *Massachusetts Quilts*, esp. 25–37; Baumgarten, *What Clothes Reveal*; and Tandy Hersh, "18th Century Quilted Silk Petticoats Worn in America," *Uncoverings* 5 (1984). In *Clothing and Fashion*, see Mary D. Doering, "Petticoats, 1715–1785" and "Petticoat Hoops and Side Hoops, 1715–1785," 1:216–220; and Mackenzie Anderson Sholtz, "Quilted Garments, 1715–1785," 1:233–235. Robert Campbell's *London Tradesman* provides contemporary insight into the business of making petticoats.

13. A cache of 1730s quilted petticoats survives at various National Trust (UK) sites, including Snowshill Manor and the Victoria and Albert Museum. American collections with similar items include Colonial Williamsburg (Accession #1951-445), the Museum of Fine Arts, Boston (Accession #47.1022), the Connecticut Historical Society (Accession #1959.54.2), and Historic Deerfield. Textile holdings at the latter include a quilted silk petticoat, with a lining of glazed worsted wool, made by Rebecca Kingsbury of Sharon, Massachusetts, circa 1730 to 1740, and a quilted silk petticoat probably from Southeastern Connecticut, circa 1750. Both are discussed in Lynne Z. Bassett's *Telltale Textiles: Quilts from Historic Deerfield* (Deerfield: Historic Deerfield, 2003), 7, 12. Historic Deerfield also has a "mock" quilted petticoat (Accession #HD F.597)—meaning that there is an impression of quilting but no actual stuffing or wadding between layers—dated in the 1700–1750 span.

14. There are many sources available that provide detailed and comprehensive studies of the prevailing sil-

houettes of women's clothing given in broad strokes here. Recommended in-depth works include two of Norah Waugh's foundational books, *Corsets and Crinoline* (London: Routledge, 1954) and *The Cut of Women's Clothes* (Routledge, 1968); Kathleen A. Staples and Madelyn Shaw's *Clothing through American History: The British Colonial Era* (Santa Barbara, Calif: Greenwood, 2013); Baumgarten's *What Clothes Reveal*, mentioned above; and Aileen Ribeiro's *The Art of Dress: Fashion in England and France, 1750–1820* (New Haven: Yale University Press, 1995). The *Clothing and Fashion* encyclopedia presents many relevant entries, including "Mantua Dress, 1600–1714," "Women's Dress and Fashion, 1600–1714," and "Women's Dress and Fashion, 1715–1785," as well as those on specific types of gowns. Readers can also find very handy illustrations with reliable explanations on museum websites, chief among them the Heilbrunn Timeline at the Metropolitan Museum of Art website: www.metmuseum.org/toah/. The timeline presents many relevant garments from the museum's collections; some drawn upon for this chapter are "Eighteenth-Century Silhouette and Support," by Jessica Glasscock; "Mantua, late 17th century, British," accession #33.54a–c; "Robe à la Française, ca. 1765, European," accession #2001.472; and "Robe à l'Anglaise, ca. 1770, American or European," accession #C.I.37.66a. For a helpful overview of court attire over the centuries, see "Court Dress" by Joanna Marschner, senior curator at Historic Royal Palaces, Kensington Palace, published on the LoveToKnow website: https://fashion-history.lovetoknow.com/fashion-history-eras/court-dress.

15. See also Baumgarten, *What Clothes Reveal*, 88–93, and Janea Whitacre, "Mantua Maker, 1715–1785," in *Clothing and Fashion*, 1:169–171.

16. "A Satire on Women's Dress, 1754," *Boston Evening Post*, February 4, 1754. Earlier printings that can be identified include the *Caledonian Mercury* (Edinburgh, Scotland), October 8, 1753, and *Universal Magazine*, 1753. The latter is documented by Alison R. G. Fairhurst in her Ph.D. thesis, "The Materials, Construction, and Conservation of Eighteenth-Century Women's Shoes," University of Lincoln, 2015.

17. For Addison and the trial of the hooped petticoat and for the *Tatler* and the agency of women, see Erin Mackie, ed., *The Commerce of Everyday Life*, 483.

18. For more on the cultural debates over hoops in Eng-

land and America, see Kimberly Chrisman, "Unhoop the Fair Sex: The Campaign against the Hoop Petticoat in Eighteenth-Century England," *Eighteenth-Century Studies* 30 (1996): 5–23; and Kate Haulman, "Fashion and the Culture Wars of Revolutionary Philadelphia," *William and Mary Quarterly* 62 (2005): 625–662. Haulman's *Politics of Fashion in Eighteenth-Century America* is an indespensible study of the relationship of gender and power over the course of the century.

19. Silence Dogood [Benjamin Franklin], *New-England Courant*, June 4–11, 1722. For more on Franklin's letter, see Silence Dogood, essay 6 ("Sir, Among the many reigning Vices of the Town . . .") in the Collections section of the Massachusetts Historical Society website: www.masshist.org/database/642.

20. To the Author of the New-England Courant, *New-England Courant*, August 13–20, 1722, p. 1.

21. *New-England Courant*, August 10–17, 1724, p. 2.

22. For regional information on women shopkeepers, see Jean P. Jordan, "Women Merchants in Colonial New York," *New York History* 58 (1977): 412–439; Jacqueline Barbara Carr, "Marketing Gentility: Boston's Businesswomen, 1780–1830," *New England Quarterly* 82 (2009): 25–55; and Eleanor Kelley Cabell, *Women Merchants and Milliners in Eighteenth Century Williamsburg*, Colonial Williamsburg Foundation Library Research Report Series—0192, Colonial Williamsburg Foundation Library (Williamsburg, 1990), available online through the Colonial Williamsburg Digital Library at www.colonialwilliamsburg.org/learn/research-and-education.

For more on Henrietta Maria East Caine, as well as the successful Boston shopkeeper Elizabeth Murray, see Patricia Cleary, *Elizabeth Murray: A Woman's Pursuit of Independence in Eighteenth-Century America* (Amherst: University of Massachusetts Press, 2000), 45–46, 57, 60, 62–63, 241n. The Massachusetts Historical Society holds a catalogue specifying Caine's inventory that was sold at auction in Boston in 1754. For examples of the advertisements Caine placed, see the American Antiquarian Society. For more, see Kimberly Alexander, "The Unfortunate Tale of Boston Shopkeeper Henrietta Maria East Caine, 1750s," April 17, 2014, SilkDamask, www.silkdamask.org. For Jane Gillam, a shopkeeper at the Mill Bridge who sold English goods, see the advertisements she placed between circa 1764 and November 1767, frequently in the *Boston Evening Post*. A typical lengthy ad was posted on June 9, 1766, in which she listed dozens of items including satins and calicos as well as stays. For Susanna Redken, who sold seeds as well as dry goods, see posts under her name at the website of the Adverts 250 Project: An Exploration of Advertising in Colonial America 250 Years Ago This Week, https://adverts250project.org.

23. On the topic of needlework in general, see Jane Nylander, *Our Own Snug Fireside: Images of the New England Home, 1760–1860* (New York: Alfred A. Knopf, 1993); Paula Bradstreet Richter, *Painted with Thread: The Art of American Embroidery* (Salem: Peabody Essex Museum, 2002); Laurel Thatcher Ulrich, *The Age of Homespun: Objects and Stories in the Creation of an American Myth* (New York: Vintage, 2002); and Amanda Vickery, *Behind Closed Doors: At Home in Georgian England* (New Haven: Yale University Press, 2010).

24. Susan P. Schoelwer, *Connecticut Needlework: Women, Art, and Family, 1740–1840* (Hartford: Connecticut Historical Society, 2010), 14.

25. *American Weekly Mercury* (Philadelphia), June 6–13, 1723, p. 4.

26. *Boston Gazette and Country Journal*, April 7, 1766, p. 376. A digital facsimile of this paper is available at the MHS website, in the *Annotated Newspapers of Harbottle Dorr*.

27. The term *apron* for this type of garment appears to have been used in the seventeenth century and into the early eighteenth. Changes in baptismal practices—the move away from full immersion—allowed for the better known christening dress or gown to supplant the earlier ensemble, which often included the apron, a bib, mitts, and a cap. The example embroidered by Mary Woodbury has proportions closer to a typical apron than to the square bearing cloth, also common in the seventeenth and eighteenth centuries. A conceptually similar apron is extant at the Museum of Fine Arts, Boston. For information, see Pamela Parmal, *Women's Work: Embroidery in Colonial Boston* (Boston: MFA Publications, 2012), 34–36.

28. *Proceedings of the Massachusetts Historical Society* 64 (1930–1932): 346. Mary married Dr. Benjamin Jones in March 1737. *Vital Records of Beverly, Massachusetts, to the End of the Year 1849*, 2:348, 479; findagrave.com, s.v. "Mary Woodberry Jones." After her death, her belongings were saved for her daughter, Lydia, by Dr. Jones's second and third wives.

29. For Elizabeth Bull Price's family and biography, see the *New England Historical and Genealogical Register* 49 (1895): 513; Henry Wilder Foote, *Annals of King's Chapel from the Puritan Age of New England to the Present Day* (Boston, 1882), 1:424; and J. L. Bell, "Update #3: Mysteries of the Elizabeth Bull Wedding Gown," February 12, 2013, *Boston 1775*, http://boston1775.blogspot.com. A blog post from Revolutionary Spaces, which holds the gown, provides valuable information but seems to miscalculate the wedding date: Elizabeth Roscio, "Elizabeth Bull and Roger Price: An 18th Century Love Story," June 18, 2015, *On King Street*, www.bostonhistory.squarespace.com/kingstreet. Elizabeth and Roger had at least four children. They departed Boston for England in June 1754, and she spent the rest of her life in England. The Price-Osgood-Valentine collection at the MHS documents many generations of the family, described in the collection guide at the MHS website: www.masshist.org/collection-guides/view/fa0460.

30. James Vincent, advertisement, *New England Weekly Journal*, April 7, 1729, p. 4. The reference to London appears in the introduction.

31. For information on silk weaving at Spitalfields, see Zara Anishanslin, *Portrait of a Woman in Silk: Hidden Histories of the British Atlantic World* (New Haven: Yale University Press, 2016); William Farrell, "Silk and Globalisation in Eighteenth-Century London: Commodities, People, and Connections c.1720–1800" (Ph.D. diss., University of London, Birkbeck, 2014); and "Industries: Silk Weaving," in *A History of the County of Middlesex: Volume 2, General; Ashford, East Bedfont with Hatton, Feltham, Hampton with Hampton Wick, Hanworth, Laleham, Littleton*, ed. William Page (London: Virginia County History, 1911), 132–137, available in British History Online, Institute of Historical Research, University of London, www.british-history.ac.uk/vch/middx/vol2/pp132-137.

32. It is difficult to decipher the name of the shoemaker. It could be Robert Dasson or Basson, of whom little is currently known. There was a Robert Dasson, born in 1690 in London, which would make him a prime candidate. Consultation with scholars Rebecca Shawcross, Shoe Resource Officer at the Northampton Shoe Museum (UK), and D. A. Saguto, Master Boot and Shoe Maker, Emeritus, at Colonial Williamsburg, yielded no additional information on the marking.

33. For information on the Byles family, see the finding

aid to the Byles Family Papers at the Massachusetts Historical Society: www.masshist.org/collection-guides/view/fa0314.

34. For details of the several alterations, and the dress's probable presence at the English court in 1760, see Bell, "Update #3: Mysteries of the Elizabeth Bull Wedding Gown."

35. For a general biography of Mather Byles, see Arthur Wentworth Hamilton Eaton, *The Famous Mather Byles: The Noted Boston Tory Preacher, Poet, and Wit, 1707–1788* (Boston: W. A. Butterfield, 1914).

36. Eaton, *The Famous Mather Byles*, 72. Rebecca's remains are interred in the Granary Burial Ground, No. 2.

37. The shoes and dress were purchased from Margaret Callet-Carcano, of Brussels, Belgium, in 1967. Another dress associated with the Byles family, most likely from the last quarter of the eighteenth century, is also in the collection.

Chapter 2

1. John Adams, diary, January 16, 1766, in *Diary and Autobiography of John Adams*, 1:294–295, available online in the Adams Papers Digital Edition, Massachusetts Historical Society.

2. The author wishes to thank Dane A. Morrison for sharing his in-progress research on Boylston for his book *Eastward of Good Hope: Early America in a Dangerous World* (Baltimore: Johns Hopkins University Press, 2021). A useful overview for this topic is Gary Nash's *The Urban Crucible: The Northern Seaports and the Origins of the American Revolution*, particularly the first chapter, "The Web of Seaport Life" (Cambridge: Harvard University Press, 1979).

3. The banyan originated in India, corrupted from a Gujarati term *Banya*, the preeminent caste of village or town trader. For more on its origin and its adoption in colonial Boston, see Ifran Habib, "Merchant Communities in Precolonial India," in *The Rise of Merchant Empires: Long-Distance Trade in the Early Modern World, 1350–1750*, ed. James D. Tracy (New York: Cambridge University Press, 1990), 371–399; K. N. Chaudhuri, *The Trading World of the Asia and the English East India Company, 1660–1760* (New York: Cambridge University Press, 1978), 137, 335; and Hunter, *Purchasing Identity in the Atlantic World*, 149.

4. For more information on Copley's portraiture as it relates to these topics, see Jane Kamensky, *A Revolution in Color: The World of John Singleton Copley* (New York: W. W. Norton & Company, 2017); Morrison, *Eastward of Good Hope*; Isabel Breskin, "'On the Periphery of a Greater World': John Singleton Copley's 'Turquerie' Portraits," *Winterthur Portfolio* 36, no. 2/3 (Summer–Autumn, 2001): 97–123; and Carol Troyen, "A Choice Gallery of Harvard Tories: John Singleton Copley's Portraits Memorialize a Vanquished Way of Life," *Harvard Magazine*, March–April 1997. Copley's 1766 portrait of Thomas Boylston II (1721–1798) can be viewed online at the website of the Harvard Art Museums, www.harvardartmuseums.org. His 1773 portrait of Rebecca Boylston Gill can be viewed online at the website of the Rhode Island School of Design Museum, http://risdmuseum.org.

5. Cotton Mather, *Magnalia Christi Americana; or, The Ecclesiastical History of New-England* (London, 1702), bk. 2, p. 19. First published in 1702, many editions came out in later years. This quotation appears in volume 1, page 138, of an edition prepared by Thomas Robbins and published in Hartford, Connecticut, in 1855.

6. Gov. John Leverett's buff coat was given to the MHS by John Leverett (1758–1829) on March 21, 1803. For information on the history and construction of buff coats, see Mary Doering's overview "Buff Coats" in *Clothing and Fashion*, 1:42–43.

7. Francis J. Bremer, *Congregational Communion: Clerical Friendship in the Anglo-American Puritan Community, 1610–1692* (Boston: Northeastern University Press, 1994), 309 n. 24; Louise A. Breen, *Transgressing the Bounds: Subversive Enterprises among the Puritan Elite in Massachusetts, 1630–1692* (Oxford: Oxford University Press, 2001), 117–118. A biographical overview of Thomas Rainsborough can be found on the BCW Project website, http://bcw-project.org.

8. A synopsis of Leverett's life appears on the page "John Leverett Papers" in the web presentation *Highlights from the Saltonstall Family Collections at the Massachusetts Historical Society*, www.masshist.org/features/saltonstall/john-leverett. The biographical sketch also provides links to related documents in the Society's collections, including the 1656 document from Cromwell with instructions regarding forts in Acadie, www.masshist.org/database/1923.

9. The quotation appears in John Tincey, *Ironsides: English Cavalry, 1588–1688* (Oxford: Osprey Publishing, 2002), 19. The same page also presents the argument

for lower costs. Several such coats survive in North American and British collections, including similar examples held at the Metropolitan Museum of Art and the York Castle Museum (UK), which houses the buff coat of Sir Thomas Fairfax.

10. *The Laws and Liberties of Massachusetts, 1641–1691: A Facsimile Edition*, comp. John D. Cushing (Wilmington, Del.: Scholarly Resources, 1976), 1:182.

11. This overview of Nicholas Boylston's Boston is adapted from Morrison, *Eastward of Good Hope*.

12. Nicholas Boylston purchased the building on School Street from Jacob Wendell in 1764. See Annie Haven Thwing, *The Crooked and Narrow Streets of Boston, 1630–1822* (Boston: Marshall Jones, 1920), 109; Hunter, *Purchasing Identity*, 148.

13. *Steward Clan Magazine*, April 1933, pp. 284–285. Variant spellings of surnames were not unusual in the seventeenth and eighteenth centuries, when regularized spelling was not observed as keenly as it is today. MHS curator Anne Bentley provided the explanation for the large size of the wallet.

14. Samuel Pepys, diary, October 8, 1666: "The King hath yesterday in Council declared his resolution of setting a fashion for clothes, which he will never alter. It will be a vest, I know not well how; but it is to teach the nobility thrift, and will do good." Pepys's extensive and detailed journal is a critical resource for information about English culture, and especially London, in the seventeenth century. A number of print editions have been published, but the most accessible is the web-based edition at www.pepysdiary.com. For a general overview of the vest and the waistcoat, see *Clothing and Fashion*, 1:281–282.

15. Pepys, diary, October 15, 1666.

16. For a thorough, albeit somewhat antiquated, recounting of William Tailer's life, see David Clapp, *The Ancient Proprietors of Jones's Hill, Dorchester* (Boston, 1883).

17. For a biography of Andrew Oliver, Jr., see *Sibley's Harvard Graduates*, 12:455–461.

18. The details about the construction of the Bromfield wig et al., and their historical context, were provided by Elizabeth Myers, Master Wigmaker at Historic Trades, and her colleague Regina Blizzard, who examined all of the pieces. Documentation via email, Elizabeth Myers to Anne E. Bentley, August 3, 2018.

19. Eliza Susan Quincy, September 1816, Journal, Quincy Family Papers, 1639–1930, MHS; Henry Bromfield Rogers, quoted by Daniel Denison Slade, "A New England Country Gentleman in the Last Century," *New England Monthly Magazine*, March 1890, p. 19. The article does not give a location for the "recent memoranda" that Rogers apparently wrote. Like similar things of the time, it may have been assumed the reader would understand the papers to still be in the family's possession.

Bromfield's clothing choices reveal an important truth about the material culture of early America: although frequently absent in the study of historic costume, outdated, reused, and recycled clothing were a common presence, whether in urbane cities or bucolic hamlets. An unwillingness to discard outdated clothing, for whatever reason, has made it possible for us to have this kind of collection of items available today.

20. The level of finished tailoring suggests construction in North America rather than London, although that could be related to cost rather than skill by this date.

21. For a biography of Peter Oliver, see *Sibley's Harvard Graduates*, 8:737–763.

22. A facsimile of Washington's original manuscript of his "Rules" appears on the website of the Washington Papers editorial project at the University of Virginia. Rule 54 is at the top of page 6: http://gwpapers.virginia.edu/documents_gw/civility/civil_06.html.

23. For a short biography of Jacky Custis and his relationship with his stepfather, see Mary V. Thompson, "John Parke Custis," in the *George Washington Digital Encyclopedia*, George Washington's Mount Vernon, www.mountvernon.org/research-collections/digital-encyclopedia.

24. For information on boys' clothing and the practice of breeching, see Linda Baumgarten, *What Clothes Reveal*, 161–168.

25. Amanda Vickery documents this division of accounts in "His and Hers: Accounting for the Household," chapter 4 of her book *Behind Closed Doors*. This extensive study of eighteenth-century account books, day books, and diaries sheds light on the finances of wealthy English households, which seems also to correlate with the evidence from Washington's papers.

26. George Washington to Charles Lawrence, August 10, 1764, in *The Papers of George Washington: Colonial Series*, ed. W. W. Abbot and Dorothy Twohig (Charlottesville: University Press of Virginia, 1983–1995), 7:321–323. All Washington Papers volumes cited

hereafter by series abbreviation and subseries title (*PGW: Series*), volume, and page numbers. All quotations from the Washington Papers volumes also appear in the digitized contents of this edition at Founders Online: Correspondence and Other Writings of Seven Major Shapers of the United States, administered by the National Archives and Records Administration and the University of Virginia Press, https://founders.archives.gov.

Washington's choice of colors for the livery reflects the family arms, as per an order he placed with a London merchant a decade previous: "I wou'd have you choose the livery by our Arms; only, as the Field of the Arms is white. I think the Cloaths had better not be quite so. but nearly likely the inclosd. The Trimmings and Facings of Scarlet, and a Scarlet Waistcoat the cloath of wch to be 12/6 pr yd. If Livery Lace is not quite disus'd, I shoud be glad to have these Cloaths Laced. I like that fashion best." Enclosure: Invoice [to Richard Washington], December 6, 1755, in *PGW: Colonial*, 2:208–209.

27. We find additional insights into Washington's thoughts on dress and decorum in surviving fragments of his attire at the Mount Vernon historic site and materials scattered in other collections. His correspondence also includes many letters to and invoices from tradesmen and brokers, domestic and in England, full of details regarding his orders for clothing and shoes for himself, his family, and the enslaved men and women on his plantation. See for example these correspondents: Charles Lawrence, Thomas Gibson, and Cary and Co., his brokers in England. Of a different nature but also interesting are his many letters during the Revolution specifying uniforms for officers in the Continental Army and wearing apparel for the soldiers.

28. George Washington to Charles Lawrence, June 20, 1768, in *PGW: Colonial*, 8:98–99. A year earlier, Washington sent this order: "I.nclosd is a Measure for Breeches, by which please to send me a pair of black silk Knit ones—I shoud be glad also to have sent me a Sartout great Coat fashionably made of good Cloth. . . . let the Breeches have cool linings fit for Summer wear and a side pocket." He followed this with "a fashionable Suit of Cloth Cloaths which you are desired to make for Master Custis (who is about 14 Yrs of age & tolerably well grown) and to send them along with the above things of mine." GW to Charles

Lawrence, July 20, 1767.

29. George Washington to Thomas Gibson, July 15, 1772, in *PGW: Colonial*, 9:62–63. All transcriptions appear as they do in the edition.

30. George Washington to John Didsbury, July 15, 1772, in *PGW: Colonial*, 9:61. The sartorial mentorship that Washington provided Jack Custis was reflected years later in his correspondence with his nephew George Steptoe Washington, to whom he sent "advisory hints" in 1789. See George Washington to George Steptoe Washington, March 23, 1789, in *PGW: Presidential*, ed. Dorothy Twohig (Charlottesville: University Press of Virginia, 1987), 1:438–441.

31. According to the *Maryland Journal and Baltimore Advertiser* of May 8, 1789, "We hear from New-York, that our beloved and illustrious President was proclaimed in a Suit of Broadcloth manufactured in the State of Connecticut. We hope, from this laudable Example in the first and best of Men, that we shall soon see Industry and Economy fashionable in the United States. National Dresses and Manners, as well as Principles, are absolutely necessary to our becoming an independent People."

Chapter 3

1. Mount Vernon has in its collections a brown broadcloth suit of George Washington's that may be the one from his inauguration. An image and details are available in the Collections section of the Mount Vernon website, https://emuseum.mountvernon/objects/1302/suit.

2. George Washington to Henry Knox, January 29, 1789, in *PGW: Presidential*, 1:260–261. An editorial note with this transcription includes considerable information about the suit cloth and the Hartford manufacturer, including this: "Writing in the *Federal Gazette*, a 'Philadelphia Mechanick,' probably inspired by Wadsworth's campaign, wrote that a 'PASSION for encouraging American manufactures has at last, become fashionable in some parts of our country. To render it more general and useful, I beg leave to propose, that the gentlemen who are, or shall be, elected to serve in the Senate or House of Representatives of the United states as also the President and Vice president, should all be clothed in complete suits of American manufactured cloth, on the approaching fourth of March' (reprinted in the *Connecticut Courant* [Hartford], 19 Jan. 1789)."

3. Knox to Washington, February 12, 16, 19, March 5, 1789, in *PGW: Presidential*, 1:291, 316, 322–323, 450–451. In reply to the February letters, Washington wrote on March 2 to acknowledge that he had received the first shipment of Hartford cloth, saying that it "is come safe, and exceeds my expectation." *PGW: Presidential*, 1:353–354.

4. For a general history of the HWM, see Chester McArthur Destler, "The Hartford Woolen Manufactory: The Story of a Failure," *Connecticut History Review*, no. 14 (June 1974): 8–32, available online via JSTOR, https://www.jstor.org/stable/44369816. For the promotional campaigns particularly, see pages 11–15.

5. Washington to Daniel Hinsdale, April 8, 1789, in *PGW: Presidential*, 2:41–42. Hinsdale's note to Washington is dated March 23, 1789, in *PGW: Presidential*, 1:433–434. The Washingtons did continue to purchase HWM cloth, and George also visited the manufactory in October 1789. See Destler, "The Hartford Woolen Manufactory," 18; and George Washington, diary, October 20, 1789, in *The Diaries of George Washington*, ed. Donald Jackson and Dorothy Twohig (Charlottesville: University Press of Virginia, 1979), 5:448–488.

6. There is a substantial body of scholarship on the power of "the politics of fashion," many of which have informed this work, including Haulman, *The Politics of Fashion in Eighteenth-Century America*; Eacott, *Selling Empire*; Jennifer Van Horn, *The Power of Objects in Eighteenth-Century British America* (Chapel Hill: University of North Carolina Press, 2017); Marla Miller, *The Needle's Eye: Women and Work in the Age of Revolution* (Amherst and Boston: University of Massachusetts Press, 2006); Beverly Lemire and Giorgio Riello, eds., *Dressing Global Bodies: The Political Power of Dress in World History* (New York: Routledge, 2020); Styles, *The Dress of the People*.

7. Scholars such as T. H. Breen have documented this history in great depth. Some also trace it back to at least the 1750s, arguing that voices rose in protest against luxury imports even before the offensive tariffs and called on colonial consumers to purchase items made locally. T. H. Breen, *The Marketplace of Revolution: How Consumer Politics Shaped American Independence* (New York: Oxford University Press, 2005), 23.

8. *Newport Mercury*, August 27, 1764. In her *Politics of Fashion in Eighteenth-Century America*, Haulman delivers an in-depth study of the complexities, and sometimes apparent contradictions, in social attitudes about luxury, consumption, and gender.

9. *New Hampshire Gazette*, September 7, 1764.

10. Along with the *Newport Mercury* for December 24, 1764, see also the *New York Mercury* for December 3 and 24. The society offered one such expedient in the form of subsidies for domestic goods, including an award of ten pounds for "the best made 100 Pair of Womens Shoes, the Soles to be of Leather tanned in this Province, and covered with Stuff [*worsted wool*]."

11. *Boston Gazette*, January 21, 1765. For an overview of linen production, see Donna C. Parker, "Use of Flax in America" (2007), DLSC Faculty and Publications, Paper 5, TopSCHOLAR®, WKU Libraries, Western Kentucky University, http://digitalcommons.wku.edu/dlsc_fac_pub/5.

Many of the terms for textiles that were familiar to an eighteenth-century reader are probably unfamiliar to most people today. Bengals, for example, were any silk or cotton textile produced in Bengal, India, and exported via the East India Company. S. William Beck's *The Draper's Dictionary. A Manual of Textile Fabrics: Their History and Applications* (London: The Warehousemen and Drapers' Journal Office, 1882) is a useful source for deciphering textile terms and their use in contemporary diaries, newspapers, and literature.

12. *Boston Gazette and Country Journal*, November 23, 1767, p. 3. See, below, the story of William Dawes's wedding for more about this venture.

13. Isaac Vibird's letter describing the incident is in the *Boston Gazette and Country Journal*, February 19, 1770, p. 3.

14. *Boston Evening Post*, January 14, 1765. For sources for the Lynn shoe industry, see Nancy E. Rexford in *Women's Shoes in America, 1795–1930* (Kent: Kent State University Press, 2000), 9–10; Paula Bradstreet Richter, "Following the Footprints of the Past: The Shoe Collection of the Essex Institute," and Jeffrey A. Butterworth, "Simply Stupendous: A Century of Exhibition Shoes, 1839–1939," *Essex Institute Historical Collections* 127 (1991): 115–160; Lewis and Newhall, *History of Lynn*; and Fred Gannon, *A Short History of American Shoemaking* (Salem: Newcomb & Gauss, 1912). See also the Lynn Museum archives.

15. See the discussion of shoemaking in the *Essex Anti-*

quarian 5 (March 1901): 67–68.

16. On the emerging scholarship around economic self-sufficiency in early households, see James A. Henretta, "Families and Farms: Mentalité in Pre-Industrial America," *William and Mary Quarterly* 35, no. 1 (January 1978): 3–32; James T. Lemon, "Comment on James A. Henretta's 'Families and Farms: Mentalité in Pre-Industrial America,'" *William and Mary Quarterly* 37, no. 4 (October 1980): 688–696; James A. Henretta, "'Families and Farms: Mentalité in Pre-Industrial America': Reply," *William and Mary Quarterly* 37, no. 4 (October 1980): 696–700; T. H. Breen, "Back to Sweat and Toil: Suggestions for the Study of Agricultural Work in Early America," *Pennsylvania History: A Journal of Mid-Atlantic Studies* 49, no. 4 (October 1982): 241–258; Michael Merrill, "Putting 'Capitalism' in Its Place: A Review of Recent Literature," *William and Mary Quarterly* 52, no. 2 (April 1995): 315–326; Ulrich, *The Age of Homespun*; Chad William Timm, "Hunting for the Market Economy: Using Historiographical Debates to Critique the Evolution of the Market Economy and Capitalism," *Radical Teacher*, no. 79, Miscellany (Fall 2007): 13–18.

17. For a general history of England's worsted wool industry, see John James, *History of the Worsted Manufacture in England* (London: Frank Cass & Co, Ltd., 1968).

18. For the Byles family letters, correspondence, and related materials, see the guide to the family papers at the MHS: www.masshist.org/collection-guides/view/fa0314. The primary biographical sources for Mather Byles, Sr., are Eaton, *The Famous Mather Byles*, and *Sibley's Harvard Graduates*, 7:464–493. J. L. Bell provides useful context for, and skepticism regarding, a quotation attributed to Mather Byles to the effect that he considered the American Revolution the rule of "three thousand tyrants": "Mather Byles, Sr., and 'three thousand tyrants,'" March 11, 2007, *Boston 1775*, http://boston1775.blogspot.com/2007/03/mather-byles-sr-and-three-thousand.html.

19. Abigail Adams to John Adams, July 16, 1775, in *AFC*, 1:249.

20. Abigail Adams to John Adams, June [16?], 1775, in *AFC*, 1:219. For an in-depth discussion of Abigail's business dealings, see Woody Holton, *Abigail Adams* (New York: Atria Books, 2010), esp. 149–155.

21. Abigail Adams to John Adams, July 16, 1775. By late October, she reported the continued increase in prices: "the price of one paper now amounts to what we used to give for a whole Bundle." Abigail Adams to John Adams, October 25, 1775, in *AFC*, 1:314.

22. Abigail Adams to John Adams, May 1, 1780, in *AFC*, 3:335.

23. Abigail Adams to John Adams, December 9, 1781, in *AFC*, 4:258; Abigail Adams to John Adams, July 17, 1782, in *AFC*, 4:346. The December 1781 letter also demonstrates Abigail's sophisticated command of the trading landscape: "There is nothing from Bilboa that can be imported with advantage, hankerchiefs are sold here at 7 dollers & half per dozen. There are some articles which would be advantageous from Holland, but Goods there run high, and the retailing vendues which are tolerated here ruin the Shopkeepers. The articles put up, by the American House were better in Quality, for the price than those by the House of de Neufvilla."

24. Writing to her son John Quincy Adams from London in 1785, Abigail described her first presentation at Court the previous week: "I had vanity enough to come a way quite self satisfied, for tho I could not boast of making an appearence in point of person or richness of attire with many of them—the latter I carefully avoided the appearence of, yet I know I will not strike my coulours to many of them." Abigail Adams to John Quincy Adams, June 26, 1785, in *AFC*, 6:196.

25. Recent in-depth biographies of John Hancock include William M. Fowler's *The Baron of Beacon Hill: A Biography of John Hancock* (Boston: Houghton Mifflin, 1980) and Harlow G. Unger's *John Hancock: Merchant King and American Patriot* (New York: John Wiley & Sons, 2000). There are no recent and few older book-length biographies of Dorothy Quincy Hancock Scott. One of the few options is Ellen C. D. Q. Woodbury's *Dorothy Quincy, Wife of John Hancock* (Washington: The Neale Publishing Company, 1901).

26. "Ransack" appears in John Hancock to Dorothy Quincy Hancock, March 10–11, 1777, which also includes several references to the "Waggoners." A transcription of the letter quoted here was first published by Abram English Brown in *John Hancock, His Book* (Boston: Lee and Shepard Publishers, 1898), 216–218. Along with the transcription, Brown noted that the original manuscript letter was then "in possession of Mrs. William Wales" (216), adding also

that this letter, "given to Mrs. William Wales by Mrs. Hancock, has never before been published" (218). He identified Mrs. Wales as "a grandniece of Mrs. Dorothy Hancock" (6), and genealogical research confirms that Dorothy's brother Dr. Jacob Quincy (b. 1734) had a granddaughter Elizabeth Ann Quincy (b. 1809) who married William Wales of Dorchester (see the microfilm guide to the Quincy, Wendell, Holmes, and Upham Family Papers, available at the MHS website). According to records from Forest Hills Cemetery, she lived to 1905. So far no evidence that the original manuscript still survives has been found. John continued these topics in a separate letter composed on March 11, also printed in Brown, *John Hancock, His Book*, 218–220.

The items in Revolutionary Spaces' Old State House collection had probably been passed down to John and Dorothy from the elder Hancocks, Thomas and Lydia Henchman. Items identified as belonging to Dorothy Quincy Hancock in the Old State House collection include her wedding shoes (Dorothy Hancock Wedding slippers, Gresham, London, Catalog #0064.1887.002, Lent by Frederick F. Hassam) as well as other shoes from London makers (Catalog #1887.0093A-B, #1942.0006), her quilt (Catalog #1911.0023, Gift of Mrs. Frank E. Peabody), her fan (Catalog #1930.0004, Gift of George B. Dexter), and a tablecloth (Catalog #1918.0012, Gift of Mrs. Katherine S. P. Nicholson). The Old State House collection also includes several garments said to have belonged to John Hancock, including breeches, a coat, a waistcoat, and two shirts, as well as a snuffbox and two pocketbooks.

One pair of shoes in Revolutionary Spaces' Old State House collection is associated with the wedding per family tradition. A dress fragment in the collection of Historic Deerfield, Deerfield, Massachusetts, may be from her wedding dress.

Items held by the MHS are mostly household goods not associated with textiles and personal adornment and grooming. Among the latter, however, are several knee buckles believed to have belonged to John and a comb (Hair 03.066) described as "Tortoiseshell comb, with fine teeth and a handle; in green leather case with a clear top. Possibly a child's or moustache comb. Cabinet book entry reads 'shell whisker-comb of J.H.'"

27. Several collections related to the Dawes family are housed at the MHS, specified in notes 28 and 35 below. For pertinent textile holdings, contact the Society's curator or reference librarians.

28. Information about Dawes is included in David Hackett Fischer's *Paul Revere's Ride* (Oxford: Oxford University Press, 1994). A few published titles treat Dawes specifically, such as C. Burr's *William Dawes: First Rider for Revolution (A Bicentennial History of the Midnight Ride, April 18–19, 1775)* (n.p.: Historic Gardens Press, 1976) and Henry W. Holland's *William Dawes and His Ride with Paul Revere: An essay read before the New England Historical Genealogical Society on June 7, A.D. 1876; to which is appended a genealogy of the Dawes family* (Boston: J. Wilson and Son [printers], 1878).

The holdings of the MHS include multi-generational manuscript collections related to the Dawes family, including the William Dawes account book, 1788–1799 (Ms. N-2321), the William Dawes papers, 1727–1814 (Ms. N-1104), the William Dawes papers, 1778–1900 (Ms. S-513), the William Dawes papers II, 1806–1850 (Ms. N-1105), and the Turner-Dawes family papers, 1802–1980 (Ms. N-2407). For information about artifacts and textiles, which are catalogued separately, contact a reference librarian or the curator.

29. Non-importation agreement, July 31, 1769 (Mss. Large 1769 July 31), MHS. A synopsis of the account book and its context appears in the MHS blog entry "New Acquisition: William Dawes Account Book," by Susan Martin, November 16, 2010, *The Beehive*, at the MHS website.

30. As quoted in J. L. Bell, *The Road to Concord: How Four Stolen Cannon Ignited the Revolutionary War* (Yardley, Pa.: Westholme, 2016), 67.

31. *Boston Gazette*, November 23, 1767.

32. Listed as Textiles—Fabrics 036 in the MHS catalogue. Camille Breeze of Museum Textile Services confirmed through fiber analysis that the piece was of woven cotton, not linen as originally thought. Assessment Report from Museum Textile Services, December 19, 2016, Item #5.

33. Scholars who have investigated needlework signatures include Susan Schoelwer, who cites examples on bedcovers, such as that of Thankful Stanton Williams (1820) and linens, such as a pillowcase by Clarissa Treadwell Perry (ca. 1830), in her *Connecticut Needlework*, 148, 160; and Linda Baumgarten, who

looks at a petticoat signed with initials and a baby's cap inscribed with the child's name in a Hollie-point needlework insertion, in her *What Clothes Reveal*, 89, 160. Other useful sources for this topic include Ulrich's *The Age of Homespun* and Richter's *Painted with Thread*.

34. Lydia the mother died in 1760, a date that is too early for this kind of woven cotton piece. Lydia who wed William in 1795, two years after Mehitable passed away, lived till 1809. This is possible, but the museum donor records for the items accessioned from the Dawes family cast doubt on it. The blue-and-white checked square, silk muff, and William Dawes's document bag all came to the MHS through the branch of the family headed by Hannah Dawes Goldthwait Newcomb.

35. For papers of Hannah Dawes Newcomb, especially her account book, see William Dawes Papers II (Ms. N-1105). For a detailed genealogy of William's offspring, see Holland, *William Dawes and His Ride with Paul Revere*, 82–95.

36. Modern research on this kind of "cottage industry" domestic production, sometimes also known as "outwork," began to emerge in the 1980s and 1990s, exemplified especially in the scholarship of Thomas Dublin and Mary H. Blewett. Among the key publications of these two historians are Dublin's *Transforming Women's Work: New England Lives in the Industrial Revolution* (Ithaca: Cornell University Press, 1994), especially chapter 1, "Women and Rural Outwork"; and Blewett's *Men, Women, and Work: Class, Gender, and Protest in the New England Shoemaking Industry, 1780–1910* (Urbana: University of Illinois Press, 1988). We can also see this work as a form of the "industrious revolution" in Great Britain and France that Giorgio Riello describes in his *Cotton*. Riello believes that the "industrious revolution" developed as a response to a consumer revolution, positing that individuals were willing to do extra work to purchase more goods. That term can be applied to Hannah's concern, as well.

37. For these two personal histories, see Laurel Thatcher Ulrich, *A Midwife's Tale: The Life of Martha Ballard, Based on Her Diary, 1785–1812* (New York: Vintage, 1990), and Jerald Brown, *The Years of the Life of Samuel Lane, 1718–1806: A New Hampshire Man and His World* (Hanover, N.H.: University Press of New England, 2000).

38. Harvard University holds a letter that Lucretia's niece Hannah Newcomb wrote to her in 1821: Fields, James Thomas, 1817–1881, collector. James Thomas Fields collection of additional autographs, 1750–1941. Newcomb, Hannah. A.L.s. to Lucretia Dawes; Keene, 8 Apr 1821. MS Am 1745.3 (7). Houghton Library, Harvard University, Cambridge, Mass. A digital facsimile is available at the library's website, https://nrs.lib.harvard.edu/urn-3:FHCL. HOUGH:37108643.

39. The Museum of Fine Arts, Boston, holds a small cotton reticule with whitework embroidery believed to be Hannah Newcomb's own handwork. Accession #09.367.

Chapter 4

1. For more information about the painting and the area it depicts, see the description at the MHS website on the item page "State Street, 1801" at www.masshist. org/database/42.

2. The "old-fashioned" clothing is also an indicator of economic status. Those who are seen working in Marston's painting—rather than strolling, chatting, or window shopping—are, not surprisingly, wearing older but serviceable garments.

3. For context on the association between the republican ideals of the Revolution and Greco-Roman aesthetics, see Bernard Bailyn, *The Ideological Origins of the American Revolution* (Cambridge: Harvard University Press, 1967), 22–26; John W. Danford, "'Riches Valuable at All Times and to All Men': Hume and the Eighteenth-Century Debate on Commerce and Liberty," in *Liberty and American Experience in the Eighteenth Century*, ed. David Womersley (Indianapolis: Liberty Fund, 2006), 325–330; David L. Barquist, "'The Honours of a Court' or 'the Severity of Virtue': Household Furnishings and Cultural Aspirations in Philadelphia," in *Shaping a National Culture: The Philadelphia Experience, 1750–1800*, ed. Catherine E. Hutchins (Winterthur: Winterthur Museum, 1994), 313–317; David O'Brien, "Executive Authority: Images of Leadership in Post-Revolutionary France and America," in *Jefferson's America and Napoleon's France: An Exhibition for the Louisiana Purchase Bicentennial*, ed. Gail Feigenbaum (New Orleans: New Orleans Museum of Art, 2003): 45–75.

4. Abigail Adams to Mary Smith Cranch, March 15, 1800, in *AFC*, 14:172–173. In the preceding para-

graph of this letter, Adams referenced "the Lay Preacher of Pensilvana"—Joseph Dennie, Jr.—and his March 15 article in the *Gazette of the United States* (published in Philadelphia) criticizing this trend in women's attire. Possibly the phrase "rich Luxurience of naturs Charms" is quoted from him. See *AFC*, 14:174, note 7.

5. Abigail Adams to Mary Smith Cranch, April 24, 1800, in *AFC*, 14:213.

6. Most of what is known about the history of this dress comes from Adams's granddaughter Elizabeth Coombs Adams. See figure list in front matter for details.

7. Mount Vernon acquired a set of dimity pockets attributed to Martha Washington in 1965 (Item #W-2470/A-B).

8. For information on the pocket belonging to Abigail Adams, see the "Collections Online" section at the MHS website, www.masshist.org/database/1835.

9. Barbara Burman and Ariane Fennetaux, *The Pocket: A Hidden History of Women's Lives, 1660–1900* (New Haven: Yale University Press, 2019), 57. For more information on pockets in general, see "A History of Pockets" at the Victoria and Albert Museum website, www.vam.ac.uk/content/articles/a/history-of-pockets.

10. The note by Elizabeth Coombs Adams is also in the MHS collections.

11. See Burman and Fennetaux, especially chapter two of *The Pocket*, entitled "'work'd pockets to my intire satisfaction': Making and Getting Pockets" (pp. 52–83), which focuses on the wide variety of materials and techniques used in creating pockets.

12. Burman and Fennetaux address the role of pockets in female agency in *The Pocket*, 123–128.

13. "A History of Pockets," Victoria and Albert Museum website.

14. For general information on nineteenth-century fashion, see Lydia Edwards, *How to Read a Dress: A Guide to Changing Fashion from the 16th to the 20th Century* (New York: Bloomsbury Academic, 2017); Lucy Johnston, *Nineteenth-Century Fashion in Detail* (London: Thames & Hudson, 2016); Astrida Schaeffer, *Embellishments: Constructing Victorian Detail* (North Berwick: Schaeffer Arts Costume Exhibition & Care, 2013); and numerous online sources such as those associated with the Metropolitan Museum of Art, the Victoria and Albert Museum, and the Museum of the

City of New York, among others.

15. There is a gap between the 1850s and the 1890s in terms of extant costumes at the MHS. For example, ensembles that fall into the category of high Victorian fashion with extensive trimmings, elaborate embellishments, and bustled ensembles are, for whatever reason, absent.

16. For more on these topics, see Jonathan Prude, *The Coming of the Industrial Order: Town and Factory Life in Rural Massachusetts, 1810–1860* (New York: Cambridge University Press, 1983); Edward H. Cameron, *Samuel Slater: Father of American Manufactures* (1960); Barbara M. Tucker, *Samuel Slater and the Origins of the American Textile Industry, 1790–1860* (1984); Barbara M. Tucker and Kenneth H. Tucker, *Industrializing Antebellum America: The Rise of Manufacturing Entrepreneurs in the Early Republic* (2008); Chaim M. Rosenberg, *The Life and Times of Francis Cabot Lowell, 1775–1817* (Rowman & Littlefield, 2011); Thomas Dublin, *Lowell: The Story of an Industrial City* (1992); and Ferris Greenslet, *The Lowells and Their Seven Worlds* (1946).

17. Riello, *Cotton*; Eacott, *Selling Empire*; Baumgarten, *What Clothes Reveal*; and José F. Blanco, "Cotton," in *Clothing and Fashion*, 1:329.

18. Although cotton was used extensively in New England fashion, increasing throughout the eighteenth century and into the nineteenth, the textile and costume collection held by the MHS is definitely skewed toward silk, and special occasion clothing (largely christening garments and baby caps), with stories that were important to the family members who donated them. Therefore, this particular collection does not provide an accurate picture of the extensive and widespread use of cotton textiles across all sectors of American society. For extant examples of cotton clothing, one must turn to other institutions such as Historic New England, Historic Deerfield, Colonial Williamsburg, the Metropolitan Museum of Art, the Museum of Fine Arts, Boston, and other sites to examine samples of eighteenth- and nineteenth-century cotton clothing for men, women, and children. Conversely, the manuscript collections of the MHS richly document the economic rise and political aspects of American cotton production and enslavement, in part through the papers of textile magnates such as Francis Cabot Lowell.

19. Styles, *The Dress of the People*, 109. Styles also empha-

sizes Beverly Lemire's argument for the phenomenon of the "fashion favorite," a textile that dominates the market for reasons other than an accessible price.

20. Anne Farrow et al., *Complicity: How the North Promoted, Prolonged, and Profited from Slavery* (New York: Ballantine, 2005), 6–10. See the preceding pages in *Complicity* for specific examples of fortunes born out of initial investments in the cotton trade.

21. Farrow, *Complicity*, 6–7. Farrow counted 472 mills in New England by 1860. A recent spate in historical research about the North's relationship to slavery reconsiders both the number of people who were enslaved in Northern states and the ways in which Northern economics depended upon human bondage in the South and the Caribbean. *Complicity* amply covers the topics touched on here.

22. See "Uncle Tom's Cabin: A Moral Battle Cry for Freedom" at the website of the Harriet Beecher Stowe Center, www.harrietbeecherstowecenter.org, for more information about the novel, including sales numbers in the United States and abroad. The section "Stowe's Global Impact" also describes the other popular forms the story took.

23. For example, the 2018 exhibition *Fresh Goods: Shopping for Clothing in Concord, 1750–1900*, curated by David Wood, with Jane Nylander and Richard Nylander, for the Concord Museum, presented detailed and thoughtful information about local shops in that town. Featuring twenty vignettes, the exhibition considered not only the shopping habits of area residents but also the types of shops they patronized. For additional information, contact the curator or collections manager at the Concord Museum. Historic sites such as Old Sturbridge Village and Colonial Williamsburg interpret various aspects of how eighteenth- and nineteenth-century consumers acquired textile goods.

24. Thomas and Susannah Johnson Leverett were the parents of Thomas H. Leverett and his sisters. Nineteenth-century printed sources are clear on Thomas H.'s information but a little uneven on the daughters. See *The History of Windsor County, Vermont*, ed. Lewis Cass Aldrich and Frank R. Holmes (Syracuse: D. Mason & Co., 1891), 310–311; Leverett, *A Memoir, Biographical and Genealogical, of Sir John Leverett, Knt.*, 158–159; and *Norwich University, 1819–1911: Her History, Her Graduates, Her Roll of Honor*, comp. and ed. William Arba Ellis, pub. Grenville M. Dodge (Mont-

pelier: Capital City Press, 1911), 2:165. Caroline Hallam Leverett and Harriet Leverett are not abundantly documented in these sources. In *The History of Windsor County*, Caroline is listed as one of seven children of Thomas and Susannah Johnson Leverett, but the name Harriet does not appear. Caroline and Harriet both appear in *A Memoir Biographical and Genealogical*, where they are grouped with another sister alongside the abbreviation "unm." among the other siblings.

25. Simon Goodell Griffin, *The History of the Town of Keene* (Keene: Sentinel, 1904), 623.

26. Sarah Dutton Leverett Tuttle's vital statistics were gathered from sources in the Ancestry.com database (*New Hampshire, Births and Christenings Index, 1714–1904* and *New Hampshire, Marriage and Divorce Records, 1659–1947*); from *Massachusetts Vital Records, 1911–1915* (Boston: New England Historic Genealogical Society, 2008), volume 1914/21, p. 499, digitized from original records held by the Massachusetts Archives and available at www.americanancestors.org; and a manuscript note in Sarah's hand pinned to the collar of her wedding dress, held at the MHS.

There are, in total, fourteen textiles catalogued at the MHS as having belonged to Sarah Tuttle. Ten of those are childhood garments, each attributed to one or both of her aunts Harriet Leverett and/or Caroline H. Leverett: Bodice and sleeve from a child's mourning dress, 1840 (Textiles—Leverett 013); Child's shirts (three), [183-] (Textiles—Leverett 003, Textiles—Leverett 004, and Textiles—Leverett 006); Infant's caps (two), [1835] (Textiles—Leverett 010 and Textiles—Leverett 011); Infant's dresses, 1835 (Textiles—Leverett 002 and Textiles—Leverett 019); Sleeves from an infant's dress, 1835 (Textiles—Leverett 008); Purse, 1840 (Textiles—Pocketbooks 020). The other four items catalogued are all dated in or around 1860, the year of her marriage: Collar from a wedding dress, by Laura Harris, 1860 (Textiles—Leverett 016); Dress fabric, [ca. 1866], maker unknown (Textiles—Fabrics 031); Shoes (two, not matched), by Viault-Esté, [1860s] (Shoes 003 [wedding shoe] and Shoes 004 [dancing shoe]); Sleeves from a wedding garment, by Mrs. Tarleton, ca. 1860 (Textiles—Leverett 009).

27. Thomas did not remain a widower for long: he remarried in 1841. *Vital Statistics of the Town of Keene, New Hampshire*, comp. Frank H. Whitcomb (Keene:

Sentinel Printing Company, 1905), 1:42.

28. See Rexford, *Women's Shoes in America, 1795–1930*, 11, for a description of this flood. Giorgio Riello has also written about Viault-Esté in his *A Foot in the Past: Consumers, Producers and Footwear in the Long Eighteenth Century* (Oxford: Oxford University Press, 2006), 212. Some of Empress Eugénie's shoes can be viewed by searching the catalogue of the Bowes Museum at www.thebowesmuseum.org.uk.

29. Anne Bentley, exhibition panel for *Fashioning the New England Family*, Massachusetts Historical Society, October 2018–April 2019.

30. Much of the family story as synopsized here was distilled by Hilda Pfeiffer Sharman in a typescript narrative written in 1979 and included with the family letters and papers transferred to the MHS in 1998. This chapter owes much to supplemental research undertaken in the papers, which are only partially processed as of 2021. We are grateful to these volunteers and staff members for their time and effort: Reed A. Gochberg, Agnieszka Rec, and Tess Renault.

31. Over a hundred Hartwell-Clark family textiles survive, many associated with Rachael and Hilda; most date from the mid to the late nineteenth century, but there are also more than a dozen from the early twentieth century. To view the catalogue entries created to represent these items (which were still being catalogued in 2020), search ABIGAIL, the MHS online catalogue, for "Textiles—Hartwell-Clark."

32. Rachael Hartwell Pfeiffer (hereafter RHP) to Ella Clark Hartwell (hereafter ECH), November 8, 1887 (nightgown); RHP to ECH, November 12, 1889 (letter includes a drawing of the collar), all Hartwell-Clark Papers, MHS. All subsequent references to this family's archival record will be to this collection. For other letters in which RHP requested items from home, see, for example, Albert Hartwell (hereafter AH) to RHP, July 25, 1887; ECH to RHP, November 6, 1887; RHP to ECH, November 8, 1887; ECH to RHP, January 14, 1887; RHP to ECH, March 15, 1888; and RHP to AH, January 24, 1890.

33. RHP to ECH and AH, August 22, August 24, 1894 (two letters).

34. RHP to ECH, May 26, 1892. A close read of this letter does not confirm the statement in the family note (also retained with the family collection), but it is possible that other documents in the collection do.

35. "Fashionable Garnitures," *Delineator*, December

1894, p. 774. Periodicals like the *Delineator* also kept fashion-hungry readers current on the latest styles from leading French designers such as the Houses of Worth, Doucet, or Pingat. Rachael's evening dress shows her savviness about current trends, even before she left for Europe in 1896.

36. RHP, Journal, February 14, 1893. She mentioned the same event again on March 13, 1893. In a journal entry for November 18, 1893, Rachael described another College Club reception, this one for Oliver Wendell Holmes, Sr. "I wore my white mouslin de soie over white satin," she wrote, "and took a childish pleasure in looking well."

37. RHP, Journal, May 13, April 11, 1893. Rachael met George Pfeiffer in July 1892. The vicissitudes of their relationship in the first year are apparent in the journal entries that ensue. See also Sharman's narrative, p. 2, regarding the Hartwells' misgivings as well as George's mother's unwillingness to accept Rachael into the family.

38. See, for example, Rachael's journal entries for May 8 (quotation) and 13, 1893.

39. Letter Journal (hereafter LJ) October 8, 1896 / October 10. For one of her choice descriptions of other travelers, see LJ September 27, 1896 / October 2. Because each Letter Journal encompasses multiple dated entries, that citations here reference both the "main" date for the LJ and the dateline for the individual entry referenced.

40. LJ October 6, 1896. Rachael titled this account "Little Miss Hartwell in France." See also LJ July 6, 1896, for her impression of Berlin when they first arrived. In these and subsequent transcriptions from these documents, interlineated text has been brought down to the baseline and cancellations have been deleted.

41. LJ March 18, 1897 / March 19; spelling retained as in manuscript. This entry includes some small sketches. For artists' models in Italy, see LJ April 4, 1897. For Rachael's description of the "middle, shopkeeping classes" in Zurich, where she and George spend much of their time in 1896–1897, see LJ January 23, 1897.

42. LJ January 28, 1897 / February 13.

43. LJ January 23, 1897 / January 25 (fur coat); LJ No 4, 2d [March 6, 1897 / March 7] (evening attire). For other references to the fur coat—usually just glancing—see, for example, LJ July 13, 1896, and LJ Jan-

uary 20, 1897. In a very different vein, Rachael also enjoyed describing the outfit she adopted for hiking and how people responded to it; see, for example, LJ July 28, 1896 / August 1; LJ August 9, 1896; and LJ September 8, 1896.

44. For example, see LJ July 28, 1896 / July 30 and LJ August 9, 1896.

45. LJ September 27, 1896 / October 2.

46. RHP to ECH and AH, October 10, 1896. In a letter the next month, Rachael was even more blunt about ways in which they had been ostracized. See RHP to ECH and AH, November 9, 1896.

47. AH to RHP, October 25, 1896.

48. RHP to ECH and AH, November 9, 1896; ditto, November 23, 1896; LJ October 8, 1896 / November 27.

49. LJ October 8, 1896 / November 27.

50. LJ December 8, 1896. Rachael's papers in the family collection also include many financial documents, such as receipts and account books. Though none yet have been explicitly identified for the winter of 1896 in England, there are many for London recorded in the following year.

51. For a brief history of the department store and catalogue holdings, see the description in the online catalogue of the National Archives (UK), https://discovery.nationalarchives.gov.uk/details/r/87eca1dd-51ea-4476-8857-2b41540c0822; and Marshall & Snelgrove entry in the online Label Resource index at the website of the Vintage Fashion Guild, https://vintagefashionguild.org/label-resource/marshall-snelgrove/.

52. Examples of Rachael's regular needlework are recorded in her letter journals. See, for example, mention of the collar of her blue and brown dress in Lausanne in September 1896 and George's overcoat in Paris in October the same year.

53. RHP to ECH and AH, January 20, 1897/Letter no. 1 2d vol: Zurich, [after January 11]. Rachael also detailed the cost: "I gave 8 francs ($1.72) 60 centimes a meter for the silk. A meter you remember is 39 inches."

54. RHP to ECH and AH (postcard), February 17, 1897/ Letter no 1. 2d vol.: Zurich. For embroidery example, see LJ January 28, 1897 / February 13. Rachael also occasionally noted mending articles of clothing in her travel papers; see, for example, LJ September 26, 1896; September 27, 1896; and LJ October 8,

1896 / October 11.

55. AH to RHP, March 2, 1897; ECH to RHP, March 4, 1897.

56. Edith Dimick, February 6, 1905; Theodora Chase to ECH, April 19, 1905. Many similar notes appear in the collection of condolence cards.

INDEX

FIG B.2: Benjamin Stuart pocketbook